STUDENT DEBT

The causes and consequences of undergraduate borrowing in the UK

Edited by Adrian J. Scott, Alan Lewis and Stephen E.G. Lea

First published in Great Britain in September 2001 by

The Policy Press
University of Bristol
34 Tyndall's Park Road
Bristol BS8 1PY
UK

Tel +44 (0)117 954 6800
Fax +44 (0)117 973 7308
E-mail tpp@bristol.ac.uk
www.policypress.org.uk

ISBN 1 86134 279 9

Adrian J. Scott is a research student at the University of Bath, **Alan Lewis** is Professor of Economic Psychology at the University of Bath, and **Stephen E.G. Lea** is Professor of Psychology and Deputy Vice-Chancellor at the University of Exeter.

Cover design by Qube Design Associates, Bristol.
Cover illustration of Alton Towers, by Don McPhee, reproduced by kind permission of the Syndication Department, Guardian Newspapers Ltd.
Printed in Great Britain by Hobbs the Printers Ltd, Southampton.

Thanks to mum and to dad for helping me when I needed it

Adrian

Contents

List of figures and tables

Figures

Tables

Notes on contributors

Guy Bellamy is a partner of Financial Dynamics, a leading business communications consultancy that has a specialist financial services practice. He has authored a number of financial service reports and provides consultancy to a range of international companies.

Stephen E.G. Lea is one of the founders of economic psychology in the United Kingdom and has published extensively in the field, including the comprehensive textbook *The individual in the economy* (1987, with Roger Tarpy and Paul Webley). He was the first treasurer of the International Association for Research in Economic Psychology, and editor of the *Journal of Economic Psychology* from 1991 to 1995. He is currently Professor of Psychology and Deputy Vice-Chancellor at the University of Exeter.

Will Lebens is International Business Director at Web Marketing, an online advertising agency. He was an undergraduate and postgraduate student at the University of Bath where he won a grant from NCR Corporation to specialise in the psychology of debt socialisation.

Alan Lewis is Professor of Economic Psychology at the University of Bath. His main relevant publication is *The new economic mind: The social psychology of economic behaviour*, with Paul Webley and Adrian Furnham (published by Harvester Wheatsheaf). He was editor of the *Journal of Economic Psychology* from 1996 to 2000.

Mandy Morgan graduated from the University of Bath in 1997, where she gained a BSc in Psychology. She is currently teaching at a primary school in Essex after completing a PGCE at the University of Wales in 1999.

Paul Powdrill conducted his research during his undergraduate degree in Psychology at the University of Exeter. He is currently working for the Civil Service in Cardiff and is interested in pursuing further research in the not too distant future.

Caroline E. Roberts is a research student at the London School of Economics, studying for a PhD in the Department of Social Psychology. Her research is concerned with British attitudes to European integration, focusing on the debate surrounding the single European currency. The issue touches on the psychology and symbolism of money from economic psychology, as well as on identity perspectives from social psychology.

Rino Rumiati is Professor of General and Economic Psychology at the University of Padua, Italy. His current research interests are on decision making and risk perception.

Adrian J. Scott is a research student at the University of Bath, where he has been awarded a student bursary by the Department of Psychology to complete a PhD in Economic Psychology. He is continuing his research into student debt with students who entered university after the abolition of the maintenance grant and the introduction of tuition fees.

Steve Stradling is Reader in Behavioural Aspects of Transport at the Transport Research Institute at Napier University, Edinburgh. While he was in the Psychology Department at the University of Manchester he took a break from studying driver behaviour to look at the psychological effects of debt management on university students.

Gaia Vicenzi graduated from the University of Padova, Italy, in 1999. Her final year project, investigating student debt, was carried out at the University of Exeter. At present, she is working on the psychology of the Euro and the phenomenon of tax evasion in the Italian context.

Paul Webley is Professor of Economic Psychology and Head of the School of Psychology at the University of Exeter. His main relevant publications are *The economic psychology of everyday life*, with Carole Burgoyne, Stephen Lea and Brian Young (published by Psychology Press) and *The new economic mind: The social psychology of economic behaviour*, with Alan Lewis and Adrian Furnham (published by Harvester Wheatsheaf). He is President of the International Association for Research in Economic Psychology.

Acknowledgements

The research presented in this book would not have been possible without the assistance of numerous individuals and organisations. Particular thanks for the help of Vanessa Hulland and Jeremy Leighton, of the University of Bath Graduate Office, for the efficient distribution of questionnaires; to David Cook and Zoe Young for their successful canvassing of off-duty students at the University of Manchester; to Jasmine Merli for the back translation of the Italian questionnaire; and to Christine Roland-Levy for the organisation of the French focus groups.

Results from several of the studies reported in this book have been presented at various conferences, including the annual conferences of the International Association for Research in Economic Psychology (IAREP), and the annual South-West Undergraduate Psychology Conference; thanks are due for many helpful comments made at those meetings. Thanks should also go out to the Economic and Social Sciences Research Council (ESRC), National Westminster Bank, and NCR Corporation for their invaluable financial backing.

Finally we should like to thank all the students, intending students and ex-students who willingly served as participants in the studies described in this book. It is their interest and cooperation that has made this book possible, and the best outcome of publication would be for it to lead to improvements in their welfare, or at least the welfare of the generations of students who succeed them.

Part I: Background

ONE

Introduction

Adrian J. Scott, Alan Lewis and Stephen E.G. Lea

This book brings together nine previously unpublished empirical studies examining different aspects of student debt in the UK; comparisons are also made with Italy and France. Qualitative and quantitative research methods have been used including focus groups, face-to-face interviews and questionnaire surveys. The context was that of continuing change in the arrangements for student finance, moving in the UK from a non-repayable grant-based system to a repayable loan-based one. All the UK research was conducted with students who had already entered university, or were expecting to apply to universities, after that process had begun, but prior to the abolition of the maintenance grant and the introduction of tuition fees in 1998.

Topics of investigation include student money management styles, student attitudes towards credit and debt, the psychological effects of student debt, and the nature of the student–bank relationship, all of which have implications for educational policy (and our understanding of the process of economic socialisation). The government claimed that the introduction of a loan system would encourage financial independence and responsibility among students. The findings presented in this book, however, suggest a different story, one in which students are being forced to take charge of their finances (often for the first time) without being fully aware of the repercussions of their actions. A combination of the incentives banks and lending institutions offer to encourage borrowing, a lack of money management skills, and a growing tolerance towards credit and debt result in many students owing a substantial amount of money at the end of their degree. In 1999 for example, the average graduate owed £5,286 (Barclays News Release, 2000), a figure that, for many university leavers, is likely to increase threefold by 2001 following the abolition of the student maintenance grant and the introduction of tuition fees.

Debt

It is important to clarify what is meant by 'debt' at the outset, as people have very different views on what constitutes a debt. The term 'student debt' has been adopted by researchers and politicians alike to cover all forms of student borrowing whether it be large or small, whether it be from a friend or family member, a bank, credit card or loan company, regardless of whether it can be repaid or not. When referring to debt, however, things are not so simple: there is no consensus on what constitutes debt, or what distinguishes it from credit. It might be argued that credit and debt are two sides of the same coin: if you use credit you are, by definition, in debt. But the term 'debt' is frequently considered as synonymous with 'bad debt' or 'problem debt', which introduces a negative connotation and clearly separates it from the neutrally regarded term 'credit'[1]. For this reason, the use of the term 'debt' to refer to credit use and borrowing has been avoided wherever possible. Although the linguistics of debt is touched upon in Chapters Three, Six and Eight, for a more comprehensive analysis of the psychological definition of debt refer to Lea (1999).

Consumer debt has recently become a subject of sharp interest among social scientists of several disciplines. This is not really surprising when you consider that there is currently about £150 billion of unsecured borrowings in the UK, of which about £39 billion is outstanding to credit cards; a figure that is rising year after year (Baines and Ernst, 2001). According to a recent survey of 698 young people conducted by Mintel, "Almost two-thirds of 16 to 25-year-olds are in debt with nearly a quarter of those aged between 20 and 24 owing at least £3,000" (Warwick-Ching, 2001). What is more, when considering attitudes towards credit and debt, the survey found that two thirds of young adults feel uncomfortable with 'debt' (Warwick-Ching, 2001). A number of empirical studies have been carried out by lawyers, sociologists, political scientists and economists, but more recently, a series of papers has considered questions of credit and debt from the standpoint of economic psychology, taking on a more psychological approach to the understanding of economic behaviour.

It is no accident that the empirical literature on credit use is strongly interdisciplinary. On the one hand, the borrowing and repayment of money are, by definition, economic behaviours. On the other, it is widely felt that economic factors alone are insufficient to provide a complete explanation for people's status as credit users. Both in lay and academic discussion, social and psychological factors are commonly invoked to account for variations in credit use under apparently similar economic circumstances; also, borrowings contracted for the most straightforward economic reasons may then have negative psychological consequences (for example, anxiety, depression, stress).

The life-cycle hypothesis

The research described in this book considers some of the psychological processes related to credit use in UK 'mainstream' university students, that is, those who enter university direct from school or further education college. There are two reasons for interest in the borrowing behaviour of this particular group of students. First, the financial situation of UK students has been changing rapidly, and one of the effects has been a sharp rise in student debt, so the matter is of urgent political and practical interest. Second, direct entry students are relatively homogeneous, in terms of income and necessary expenditure, which allows us to look at some theoretical questions about economic socialisation and credit use in a relatively clear light.

It is inevitable, when considering student debt, that the life-cycle hypothesis (LCH), or one of its variants, will crop up during discussion, so it is necessary to provide a brief overview early on. When considering the economic theory outlined below it is also important to realise that the welfare state fits very naturally into the framework of economic analysis (Barr, 1993). As Le Grand (1997) pointed out, the replacement of the state provision of services by 'quasi-market' provision was based on the assumption that people are motivated by their own self-interest (individuals are rational income maximisers).

Following the 'rational economic man' paradigm, economists Modigliani and Brumberg (1954) developed the LCH, which suggests that people rationally determine the amount they can consume at different periods in their life, and that the difference between income and expenditure will be the amount saved, or the amount borrowed. They proposed that when people are young (students) they will borrow to pay for consumption, when they are middle aged they will repay the money owed and save for retirement, and when they are old they will spend the money already saved (dissave). Friedman (1957) follows the same line of thought in his 'permanent income hypothesis', in which people have a notion of what their permanent income over time will be and spend accordingly[2].

Although these arguments are consistent with student reports of borrowing at university, they depend on two assumptions. First, it is assumed that studying is an 'investment' in the individual's 'human capital' and that the acquisition of new knowledge and skills will lead to above-average salaries in the future, a view that goes back at least to Becker (1974). Second, it is assumed that individuals are economically rational, in the sense that they will do whatever is to their greatest long-term economic advantage. Both of these are contentious issues. Talik (1999), for example, drew attention to the uncertain nature of the relationship between higher education and future employment and stated that it is wrong to assume that the association is either perfect or strong. Webley et al (2001) discuss the economic psychology of the choice to enter higher education in some detail and show that the 'human capital theory' outlined above is at best a partial account of the data. As for the assumption of economic rationality, it has been questioned by psychologists from the moment they started to look at economic theory (see Lea et al, 1987).

A frontal assault on rationality is probably not the best way to forward research in economic psychology (see Lea, 1994), but the kind of intertemporal choice involved in savings and debt is one of the areas where any simple version of the rationality assumption is most obviously false. For example, as Lewis et al (1980) pointed out, consumption and savings are highly sensitive to current income; or in the case of students, the availability of credit.

A revised version of the LCH, the behavioural life-cycle hypothesis (BLCH), was offered by Shefrin and Thaler (1988), who highlighted a major flaw in the assumption of rational economic man, as it applies to choices over time: people are impatient (especially in the short run) and often lack self-control. Shefrin and Thaler contended that the idea that individuals make an 'optimal consumption plan' and stick to it is erroneous, because "in real life, people realise that self-control is difficult" (Thaler, 1992, p 109). Thaler's account, however, is relatively simplistic in its departure from rational economics and its adaptation to economic psychology, and does not specify whether this realisation is inherent or acquired through experience. One of the contentions of this book is that people do have to learn their own limitations as money managers, and that as university is the first experience of financial independence for many individuals it is a time for financial learning. Unfortunately, under current UK policy this learning process leaves quite a high proportion of individuals with serious financial liabilities at the beginning of their adult lives.

Changes to student finance

Increasing reliance on loan finance among students is a widespread phenomenon in the developed world, but the changes have been particularly acute in the UK. Living expenses and tuition fees, which for 25 years or so were met completely for most students by government grants, now fall largely on students and their families. A major expansion of higher education, from a participation rate of about 10% in the 1960s to over 30% now, has coincided both with high inflation and with a period in which politics have been dominated by a perceived need to reduce public expenditure. The result has been a steady downward drift in the value of maintenance grants, the progressive replacement of the grant by a government-backed loan, and most recently, in 1998, the abolition of the maintenance grant and the introduction of tuition fees.

The student grant system was introduced in 1962 and provided financial support via a means tested maintenance grant, based on parental income, and the payment of tuition fees (Callender and Kempson, 1996). Although the expenditure of public funds on higher education rose steadily between 1962 and 1988 it failed to keep up with the increasing number of students enrolling in university, and the real value of the maintenance grant decreased year after year (McCarthy and Humphrey, 1995; West, 1994). Student loans were set up in 1990 to tackle these capital market imperfections (Glennerster, 1993) and reflected a fundamental shift in policy makers' beliefs regarding human motivation and behaviour. People were no longer viewed as 'public spirited altruists' or 'passive recipients of state largesse', but instead considered to be 'self-interested' (Le Grand, 1997). From the beginning of 1990 the maintenance grant was frozen for four years, followed by a 10% reduction in the grant each year until 1998[3]. Although banks were not prepared to lend students enough to pay the full cost of higher education (Glennerster, 1993), their role, in terms of student finance, changed during this transitional period. They started to offer financial incentives to students for opening an account and typical lending packages offered an interest free overdraft as well as a credit card facility with no annual fee.

Maintenance costs for UK undergraduates are high because few live at home: in 1998/1999 the average expenditure of a full-time student was £6,161, of which 66% was on living costs, 21% on housing costs, 12% on participation (for example, books, equipment, travel), and 1% on children (Callender and Kemp, 2000). At the same time, high levels of unemployment have made vacation jobs, the traditional standby of the impoverished student, hard to find, and students have been debarred from drawing a number of social security benefits (such as housing benefit, vacation hardship allowance). Consequently, many have to support themselves through a complex arrangement of formal and informal loans, from banks and families as well as from the government-backed Student Loans Company.

Political context

The abolition of the student maintenance grant and the introduction of tuition fees did not take place without political unrest, which has been dominated by two lines of argument. The first relates to the increasing cost of university and its impact on economically disadvantaged groups. As David Canavan, the Labour MP for Falkirk West stated, "How can they [the government] even contemplate kicking away the ladder of opportunity from so many students and future students by depriving them of grants and forcing them to pay tuition fees?" (cited in O'Leary, 1997). The other, by contrast, is based on the human capital model and considers student debt to be an investment in the future. As David Blunkett, the Education and Employment Secretary, pointed out, "We are not penalising the student at the point of entry, we are asking for a contribution at the point of reward" (cited in Sherman, 1998). It might also be argued, on the basis of other countries' experiences, that some politicians are overestimating the impact of tuition fees. In Australia, for example, demand for higher education did not fall and the participation of disadvantaged groups remained unchanged despite the reintroduction of tuition fees (Harding, 1995, cited in Varga, 1996).

Because of the topical interest in student debt, universities, student unions, banks, and the media have sponsored a number of recent survey investigations in the UK, some on quite a large scale (for example, the annual Barclays Student Debt Survey; UNITE/MORI Student Living Report, 2001). According to the Higher Education Statistics Agency the total number of enrolments at UK higher education institutes stood at 1,757,200 for the 1999/2000 academic year, which represented a 1% increase from 1998/99. It is also notable that the number of UK enrolments at UK higher education institutes has increased by 8% between 1995/96 and 1999/2000 (Statistical First Release 38, 2000)[4]. Unfortunately, these figures only consider the effect of policy on university enrolment and do little to explore the impact that policy changes are having on the experiences of the students themselves. For example, the UNITE/MORI (2001) report, based on a sample of 1,103 UK full-time university students, found that more than one third of students are seriously worried about the levels of debt they are going to incur as a result of going to university. There is still no consensus regarding the effects of abolishing the student maintenance grant and introducing tuition fees (at least on the direct entry students we are concerned with in this book), however, or whether it is even realistic to describe the loan scheme as a substitute for the grant system.

The economic psychology of student debt

Within economic psychology, discussion of student debt has focused on two main areas: student attitudes towards credit and debt (with which is linked the question of student money management strategies), and the impact of being in debt on mental health. Both have particular relevance to the studies included in this book.

Student attitudes towards credit and debt

Many of the studies reported in this book have been influenced by an early piece of research on the economic psychology of student debt, reported by Davies and Lea (1995). They looked at levels of debt and attitudes towards credit and debt in a sample of UK undergraduates. Although not all students were found to be in debt, by the third year of university two thirds of the sample were incurring some debt. This willingness to borrow has tended to be explained in terms of one of the life-cycle theories (for example, Ando and Modigliani, 1963), whereby a student borrows money while at university, a period of low income, on the basis of higher future earnings on graduation.

In addition, the study found that higher levels of debt were associated with more tolerant attitudes towards credit and debt, a trend that has also been reported with general population samples (for example, Livingstone and Lunt, 1992). But more interesting was the finding that the development of 'debt' itself and attitudes towards credit and debt took different courses: levels of debt rose most sharply between the first and second years of study, while attitudes towards credit and debt changed most between the second and third years of university. This finding led Davies and Lea to assert that, in the field of student debt anyway, attitude change follows behavioural change. They argued that this conclusion supported consistency theories of attitude change such as 'cognitive dissonance theory', which suggests that the two elements are dissonant if they do not 'fit' together (Festinger, 1957). As a result, the individual strives to reduce the 'dissonance' through either changing behaviour or altering cognition. In the context of student debt it may not be possible for individuals to change their behaviour (say, reduce their borrowings), so instead, they modify their attitude to become more tolerant towards credit and debt. Other consistency theories of attitude change, such as Bem's (1972) 'self-perception theory', which asserts that in the absence of a clear external cause people will infer their attitudes from their behaviour, also predict that attitudes will follow behaviour change.

Gender differences in levels of debt and attitudes towards credit and debt were also noted, with men being more likely to borrow, to owe more, and to have more tolerant attitudes towards credit and debt than their female counterparts. But in an environment of relative homogeneity why is it that male students are more likely to borrow and owe more than female students? Johnes (1994), who found similar differences with his sample of 1,210 university undergraduates, argued that these differences could be related back to the LCH and the lower lifetime earnings of women compared to men. This application of the LCH to individuals' day-to-day decision making has been questioned, however, and Davies and Lea suggested that it was more likely that these disparities relate to differences in the spending patterns or budgeting styles of men and women. Their view coincides with a small body of research illustrating that money management styles differ sharply and consistently according to gender, (for example, Prince, 1993) and that a weaker management style is linked to greater levels of debt (for example, Lea et al, 1995).

The impact of student debt on mental health

There appears to be a significant association between student debt, being female, and mental health problems such as anxiety and depression. Vingilis et al (1998), using a sample of 840 Canadian students, found that an individual's financial situation and gender acted as significant determinants of self-rated health. It is important to note that this finding may be culturally dependent as no gender difference was found in Singapore where the ideology was one of male dominance (Lim and Teo, 1997).

Roberts et al (1998), who found a link between financial difficulties and poor mental health in their sample of UK students, brought attention to the need to clarify the nature of the causal relationship between financial problems and poor mental health. They pointed out that the results of previous research could be interpreted in two ways: that monetary problems affect mental health, or that people with poor mental health are more likely to get into financial difficulty. Recent research, however, has suggested that there may be a third interpretation, one in which monetary value is not important. As Hesketh (1999) argued, there is a problematic dichotomy between the objective real-term value of finance and the varying subjective interpretations of students towards their finances. Rather than there being one financial experience for all students, there are many different experiences, each being determined by a combination of an individual's cultural background and economic experiences.

Hesketh (1999) built upon this idea by suggesting that there are distinct 'types' of student who respond differently to the prospect of being in debt. One group, for example, might consider student loans and bank overdrafts to be a necessary outcome of government policy and will suffer little anxiety as a result. Another group, by comparison, will experience an anxiety-reactive response to borrowing and see student debt as being imposed on them rather than a matter of choice; for them, there will be clear repercussions for the educational experience.

Structure of the book

The book aims to extend the empirical base for an understanding of student debt and its psychological causes and consequences. It is hoped that by doing this we will be able to highlight some of the main areas of concern relating to student well-being, with the view to improving the experiences of future students. The book consists of eight chapters, six of which report on previously unpublished empirical studies of student debt. The chapters have been grouped into four parts: this introduction; four chapters on the UK experience; two chapters that take an international perspective; and a final summing up[5]. The different chapters use a variety of research techniques, qualitative and quantitative. In all the empirical work, students or recent ex-students served as researchers, and played a full role in the planning of the studies and in the qualitative work. Thus, the studies reported here combine relatively 'neutral' research with an inside perspective into the student experience.

Part II: The UK experience

Mandy Morgan, Caroline E. Roberts and Paul Powdrill start with their paper entitled 'More money than sense? Investigating student money management'. They report on three independent studies, utilising focus groups, interviews and questionnaires with a combined sample of 322 undergraduates, looking at 'budgeting' and 'mental accounting' in relation to student money management. Despite the separate nature of the research, a number of common themes were identified. Overall it seemed that students were poor money managers, although women and students who viewed their income as fixed were found to be more efficient at budgeting. Most students had more than one bank account to organise their finances, but few actually did much by way of limiting expenditure during periods of financial hardship, especially when it came to socialising and alcohol consumption. Having said this, a number of different budgeting styles were distinguished, ranging from individuals who did not really make any budget plans or worry about money, to those who knew exactly how much they had available each week and made every effort to stick to a weekly limit.

Stephen E.G. Lea, Paul Webley and Guy Bellamy's paper 'Student debt: expecting it, spending it and regretting it' naturally follows on from the previous chapter as it sets out to develop a comprehensive model of student debt incorporating the notions of spending patterns and money management. Three questionnaire surveys were conducted using 659 lower sixth form (Year 12) pupils, 1,129 current university students, and 54 recent graduates. It was found that students' definitions of debt were variable, and tended not to correspond to formal financial definitions. In particular, many students did not count long-term credits such as government student loans as forms of debt. There were no direct relationships between class or family background with levels of debt. Self-reports of money management showed poorer strategies among those who owed more and many students reported money management strategies that were expenditure – rather than income – driven. There was a small but significant tendency for women to owe less money than men and in general to manage their money more effectively. Attitudes towards credit and debt were slightly more tolerant among students who had been at university longer, but all current students were much more tolerant of credit and debt than either intending students or ex-students. Intending students had very inaccurate ideas of typical student spending patterns, especially relating to social activities and alcohol expenditure, and current students tended to be unrealistically optimistic about their future earning power. The results confirm previous research, which has suggested that tolerant attitudes towards credit and debt are a consequence rather than a cause of increased credit use, and that money management strategies are an important factor in the level of debt people incur under difficult financial conditions.

Adrian J. Scott and Alan Lewis' contribution 'Student loans: the development of a new dependency culture?' builds upon the work of Lea, Webley and Bellamy (Chapter Three) by focusing on the continuation of student debt after graduation and the specific relationship between student loan use and attitudes towards credit and debt. One hundred and eighty-eight ex-students, who had graduated 16 months previously, took part in the questionnaire survey. There was very little change in the levels of debt between graduation and the time of the survey. Over three quarters of the participants had graduated with some debt and only 10% had been able to clear these; the amount owed had actually increased for those who remained in debt. Men were found to owe more than women at the time of graduation, a difference that had assuaged 16 months later, probably as a function of the higher incomes of male graduates. Attitudinally, men (compared to women) and those in debt (compared to those without debt) found credit and debt more acceptable, but student loan use was the only factor to have a significant effect on the 'acceptability of credit and debt', a finding that may have longer-term consequences. Furthermore, comments suggested that although students saw credit use as an inevitable part of university life, few had really considered the long-term consequences of the student debt they had incurred.

Steve Stradling goes on to investigate students' interpretations of their financial situation in his chapter 'The psychological effects of student debt'. Three questionnaire surveys were conducted, one with a prospective student sample (612), and the other two with current undergraduate student samples (223 and 199 respectively). Of prospective students, 81% had concerns regarding the financing of their university education, a figure that was higher for women than men. Half of the current student sample felt that financial difficulties affected their academic performance and believed that they would experience difficulties with the repayment of their student debt after graduation. Two causes of financial difficulty were identified: poor money management and unforeseen exigencies beyond their apparent control.

Students' state of mind concerning credit and debt was not best predicted by 'economic indicators' but by their 'psychological interpretations' of the situation, and it was this that presented the psychological burden of debt. The most significant factor in determining whether students viewed money owed as a burden or not was student loan use, with 84% of those who anticipated their student debt on graduation to be excessive holding a student loan, compared with only 29% of those who thought it would be at a manageable level. This finding suggests that student loan use might actually worsen the psychological burden of debt that students have during their university career and anticipate carrying after.

Part III: An international perspective

This portion of the book builds on the research reported in Part II to make some international comparisons between students in the UK and those in Italy and France. The purpose is to illuminate the UK experience and theories of credit use, by making comparisons with countries in similar economic conditions but with very different arrangements for student finance.

Gaia Vicenzi, Stephen E.G. Lea and Rino Rumiati in their paper titled 'Student attitudes towards credit and debt: a cross-national study between Italy and the UK' they compare the experiences and understanding of credit and debt in students from the UK with students from Italy (where student debt is practically unknown). Questionnaire surveys were used with two groups of students: the UK sample consisted of 121 university undergraduates and the Italian sample included 364 students as well as 89 student 'drop-outs'. In the UK, levels of debt were found to increase across year groups along with a growing tolerance towards credit and debt (in line with the findings of Lea, Webley and Bellamy, Chapter Three). In Italy, by comparison, very few students were in debt and there was no change in levels of debt according to year of study. These differences reflect 10 years of an enforced culture of borrowing in the UK where the use of credit is an unpleasant fact of life, mistrusted by those who have not yet experienced it, and increasingly tolerated by those who have to use it. In Italy, however, where credit use is unusual, it can still be seen as something the rich can afford and the rest, though they might envy it, do not aspire to.

Will Lebens and Alan Lewis round up the research in their chapter 'Are students serious bankers? The nature of the student–bank relationship in the UK and France'. Two studies into the nature of the student–bank relationship were conducted; one in the UK, where there is a legitimate need for the use of credit, the other employing samples from the UK and France (a nation that strongly discourages borrowing). Focus groups were used, 18 in total. There was strong evidence to suggest participants believed that students and banks in the UK behave towards each other in a manner contrary to their beliefs (the existence of duplicitous attitudes), which were reflective of a negative financial conscientiousness encouraged by easily accessible credit. In contrast, French students were more likely to respect the nature of banks and accept their need to make a profit.

Part IV: Summing up

The final part draws together the research reported on in this book and identifies the implications for policy: the two recurring themes of money management and student loan use are given precedence. Theoretical considerations and links to research, particularly in economic psychology, are aired as well as suggestions for future research.

Notes

[1] Lewis and Scott (1999) asked 179 school pupils, mainly aged 17 and 18, the differences between credit and debt. Of the 114 (64%) who attempted an answer, the majority (57%) viewed debt negatively compared to credit and only a small minority saw no difference between the two (7%).

[2] There have been many subsequent variations of the LCH, and between them they account for almost all the current economic theory of consumer savings and debt.

[3] This reduction in the value of the maintenance grant was compensated for by a proportional rise in the value of student loans.

[4] Such figures should be regarded with caution, as all statistics are open to interpretation.

[5] A number of statistical analysis techniques are referred to during the course of this book. They will be written in *italics* and included in the glossary (Appendix B).

Part II:
The UK experience

TWO

More money than sense? Investigating student money management

Mandy Morgan, Caroline E. Roberts and Paul Powdrill

Introduction

The primary purpose of this chapter is to establish whether the notions of 'budgeting' and 'mental accounting' are at all relevant to student money management. Previous work on student money management has been undertaken within the context of student debt, tending to concentrate on spending patterns, involvement in paid employment, and the use of credit and student loan facilities. From this research it seems that students are poor at managing money. In particular, it appears that male and female students manage their money differently, and since women generally owe less than men, it is likely that they employ more efficient money management strategies than their male counterparts.

Literature documenting the characteristics of students' money management is limited and does not provide a complete picture. Livingstone and Lunt (1992) for example commented on the importance of the overall style of money management in relation to levels of debt. They found, from a sample of 279 'ordinary Oxford residents', that those in debt were more likely to use flexible strategies, varying their budgets according to the situation and rethinking decisions if unexpected expenditures arose. Conversely, those without debt were more likely to have a general plan, which they tried to carry through regardless of circumstances. Thus, Livingstone and Lunt claimed that a flexible money management strategy is likely to encourage borrowing, masking an actual loss of control over budgeting.

It is also important to note that students represent a low-income group. As Ashley (1983) pointed out, planning expenditure and being able to account for how money is spent is particularly important for individuals with a limited income if they are to retain liquidity and minimise the amount they have to borrow in order to meet essential commitments. Similarly, Kempson et al (1994) reported that two thirds of the low-income families they interviewed managed their finances with deliberation and foresight, planning expenditure and knowing exactly how all the money was spent. Most research on the management of low incomes, however, has been based on the assumption that successful money management involves the avoidance of borrowing. It does not address the topic of budgeting from a student's perspective, where some form of credit use is often a necessity.

When considering students it is interesting to look at how they organise the resources available to them into different bank accounts and/or budget plans, and to see whether they allocate different amounts of money into so-called mental accounts. Three independent studies investigating various aspects of student money management were conducted, with particular emphasis on comparisons between the money management strategies of male and female students and more specifically, whether women adopt stricter budgeting styles than men.

Method[1]

Study 1

This study was conducted by Mandy Morgan and consisted of two phases. Phase one comprised two focus groups, one with six male students and one with six female students. In phase two, questionnaires were administered to 50 male and 50 female students. Participants were final year undergraduates from a range of academic departments at the University of Bath.

The questionnaire was divided into sections, representing the varying aspects of money management discussed in the focus groups, including spending patterns, financial priorities, and styles of money management.

Study 2

The second study was carried out by Caroline Roberts and also consisted of two phases. In phase one, 20 undergraduates were interviewed. The sample consisted of 10 first year (five male, five female) and 10 final year (five male, five female) students. In phase two, 90 undergraduates took part in a questionnaire survey; 46 were first years (24 male, 22 female) and 44 were final years (18 male, 26 female). This time, participants were from a range of academic departments at the University of Exeter.

The questionnaire consisted of five sections of questions including background details, previous borrowing experience, explicit banking procedures and 'mental accounting', styles of money management, and spending preferences.

Study 3

The final study in this chapter is that of Paul Powdrill who conducted a questionnaire survey with 100 final year undergraduates from the University of Exeter. The sample was approximately matched for gender, and again, participants were from a range of academic departments.

Similar to the previous two studies, the questionnaire was designed to look at the differing ways students manage their money, organise their income and budget their expenditure.

Results and discussion[2]

The results of the three studies will be presented and commented upon independently before common themes are drawn together in the final section of this chapter[3].

Study 1

Spending patterns

Men's monthly expenditure was found to be, on average, 80% higher than that of women. This difference was found to be the result of their higher expenditure on alcohol, food and sport, and can be seen in Figure 2.1.

Figure 2.1: Differences between men's and women's monthly expenditure

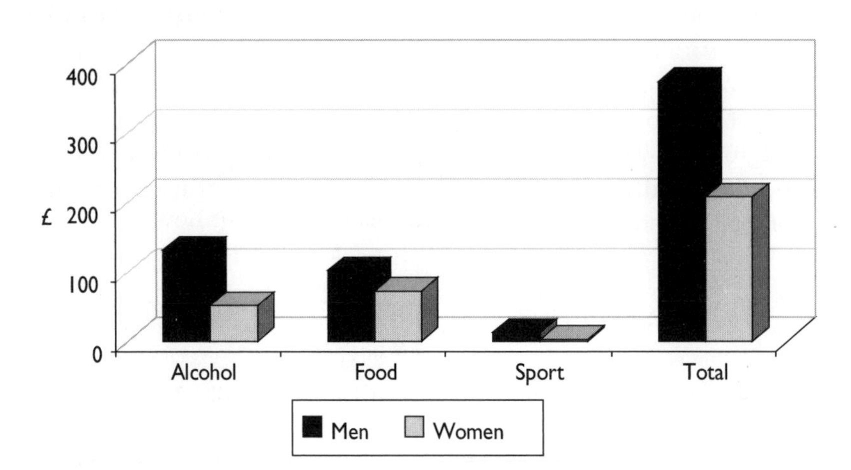

It should be noted that this finding does not coincide with the prediction of the existing literature, which suggested only a slight difference between the expenditure rates of male and female students (Callender and Kempson, 1996). It might be that the sample used was financially better off than the national student population[4], or else reflects a certain level of bravado on the part of the men in the study. The finding that men spent more than women on alcohol (£123.90 per month compared to £49.50), however, may be explained in terms of different 'reference groups'. It will not surprise anyone who is familiar with students that alcohol is an important and large part of the 'student culture', but it appears that this is more so for the male reference group than for the female one. This line of thought is illustrated by a variety of comments in the initial phase of research, including that of a male participant:

> "No I don't cut back on beer if I'm short; it's just not what you do. You cut back on other stuff but not beer. I mean, going down the pub is a must for me, and anyway my mates would think I was a bit odd if I said I couldn't go out for a few bevvies."

In contrast a woman stated:

> "I've never understood how blokes can spend 30 quid a night down the pub. I cringe if I spend more than 15. Don't get me wrong I go

out loads, but there's more to life and you've got to be sensible about spending to a certain extent."

Financial priorities

Although there was little difference in the extent to which men and women reported they would 'still go out' regardless of their financial situation, women were more careful than men about how much they would spend when money was particularly short. This approach can be further understood through the following quotes:

> "In my experience women are more likely to stay in if they haven't got any money. Or they might come out but'll be really, really careful about what they're drinking and spending." (female participant)

> "Women are more aware of how much they spend, and if they're overspending they do take action on it. Whereas we'll say, sod it, I'll spend a bit more." (male participant)

In terms of prioritising their expenditure, women were more likely to say they would pay a bill with their last £10 than were men, who were more likely to say they would spend the money on a social activity.

Styles of money management

Men and women differed in their general styles of money management. Women were more likely to use a flexible budget plan, varying according to the situation. Men, by comparison, were more likely not to use any form of budget plan, spending money as and when needed as can be seen in Figure 2.2.

This difference was apparent within the focus groups, and the following quotes from two male participants were typical:

> "... you might start the term and say, 'I can spend this amount of money this term', but you don't break it up, and say 'right I've got that for the week'. You go out and you always go out.... I think people go up to their overdraft limit and then put things on their

Figure 2.2: Differences between men's and women's money management styles

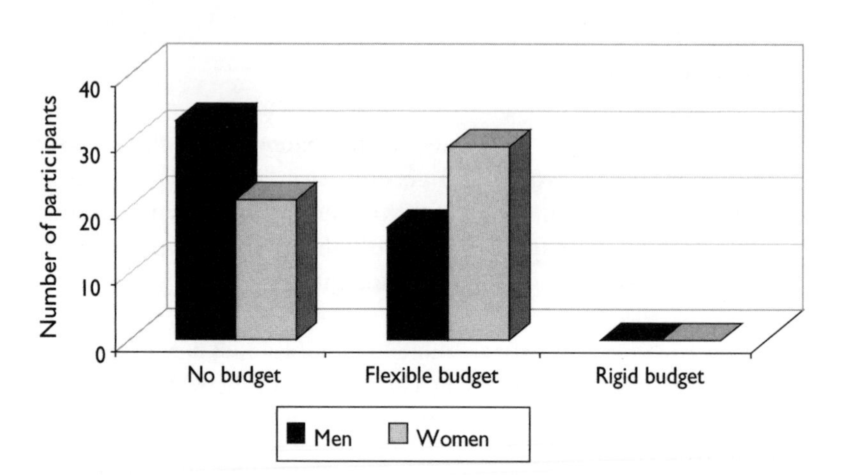

> card as well, and hope they can pay it off next time round when they get their grant or the next part of their student loan, and even delve into the Access Fund if they can. I just think nobody … well I don't budget at all, or make any attempt to."
>
> "Spend money as you need to, deal with it as it happens. That's my motto."

Female students, on the other hand, were identified as having some form of budget plan even if the plan was not well specified, as illustrated by these comments from two female participants:

> "Although I don't work to a strict weekly budget plan or anything, I have got a rough idea of how my money is spread out over a month or a term."
>
> "I've sort of got a budget I suppose. I mean, I've got a rough idea of how much I should be spending where, and I try not to be excessive with things like food."

The above quotes suggest that the money management strategies used by students do differ according to gender, and may go some way to explain why men owe more than women. In terms of the recommended student budget plan outlined by the Student Finance Office at the

University of Bath at this time, men were spending nearly 50% of the annual recommended amount for social activities on alcohol alone, every month. Women were also overspending on alcohol according to this budget plan, but by a more reasonable and realistic amount (Student Finance Office, 1996). The finding that men spent more on alcohol than women, and cut back less than women on social activity expenditures when finances were scarce, would indicate that men have to borrow in higher amounts than women in order to maintain their lifestyles. This, combined with women's propensity to curb general spending more than men when money was short, might suggest that it is a means by which female students try to minimise the amount they borrow. In terms of financial priorities men were again more likely than women to find themselves in arrears with bills, because they gave social activity expenditure precedence over more essential costs.

Although women used a flexible budget plan, which Livingstone and Lunt (1992) reported as being related to indebtedness, it seems plausible that not using any form of budget plan is going to be related to even higher levels of debt, providing another explanation of why men borrow more than women. Within the present study the finding that women had stronger money management strategies is possibly due to a greater reticence in taking on increasingly high levels of debt, which might be a reflection of the reality that their future earnings are unlikely to be as high as men's. This sentiment was expressed by participants in the initial stages of the research, and again agrees with the various life-cycle models, which claim that the amount someone is prepared to borrow is dependent on their expected future income. A female participant remarked:

> "I worry about my debts but I don't think men do. I think women worry about their financial situation because of their opportunities in the job market. Men don't need to worry so much though 'cos their salaries are probably going to be quite high."

Conversely a man stated:

> "I get money from anywhere I can. I'm not really bothered about getting into debt 'cos I know that I'll get a damn well paid job after I finish."

General trends

Significant differences were only found within four of the 31 question areas included in the questionnaire. This shows that on the whole, male and female participants' money management strategies did not differ to a great extent. What the findings did show, however, was that in general, neither male nor female students managed their money with great ability or care. Both men and women rated their money management skills as poor, neither planned for social or luxury expenditures to a great degree, and the majority reported that they did not plan for essential expenditures, but instead tried to meet these costs as and when they arose[5].

In contrast to other low-income groups, students were not found to manage their finances with deliberation and foresight. Again this may be explained in terms of one of the life-cycle models (for example, Modigliani and Brumberg, 1954). Low-income groups in the general population might not be willing to borrow much money because it is unlikely that their future earnings will allow for repayment. As a result they are inclined to plan expenditures in order to ensure that they are living within their means, and thus avoid having to borrow money (Kempson et al, 1994). Students, however, have relatively good long-term prospects in contrast to other low-income groups and as a result may be relatively willing to use credit and thus not need to manage their finances with the same care and deliberation as other low-income groups.

It was also noted that neither men nor women cut back on their expenditure to a great degree if they had recently overspent, possibly because they viewed credit use as inevitable. The following quotes from two participants illustrate this sentiment:

> "The major problem is when you look at your finances for the year you're almost in debt before you start with your fixed outgoings. So you just give up budgeting, really. You just go out and spend it all, get pissed and forget about it; and worry about it when it happens." (male participant)

> "I usually start off trying to budget and always end up forgetting about it or just not being able to keep to it because there are other things I need to buy, and then I think, 'I won't bother this time' and end up failing. So then I don't bother budgeting at all." (female participant)

Study 2

Explicit banking procedures and 'mental accounting'

For many of the participants (77%), the student bank account they opened when they first started university was not the only account they held. Often, students had either a savings account of some kind (58%) and/or another current account left over from before they started university (52%). There was also a clear tendency for the money from different accounts to be spent in different ways, with the student bank account representing the most 'liquid' form of wealth. As one participant stated:

> "I have a TSB current account, to keep the money I earn separate from my parents' money and I use it to buy things that I think my parents shouldn't – like clothes, birthday presents, travel during term time...." (female first year)

There appears to be a degree of 'mental accounting' (using different sources of money distinctly) depending on whether money was seen as 'current income' (from a government grant or parental contribution), or 'personal income' (money that the student has earned during the vacation). This hypothecation was not only reflected in the way the money was spent, but also in the explicit accounting system used: the money was kept physically separate in discrete bank accounts. Similarly, savings were treated differently, in that the money was usually viewed as a back-up, for when the student account ran low or to pay for larger items such as holidays. For example, a male final year student had a personal current account that he only used "occasionally, if things got desperate during term time". Likewise, a female first year student explained how she used her building society account as "back-up if I'm over my budget".

Styles of money management

The interviews conducted prior to the commencement of the questionnaire survey included a portion of questions relating to the ways students organised their finances and to establish how strict these strategies were. The students mentioned a variety of strategies (or non-strategies) when asked whether they made any 'budget plans' when they first started university. Examples included:

> "No, I just thought, 'I'll just see how it goes and then if it gets desperate I'll do something about it'. It's okay so far." (male first year)

> "Yes, the university sends you a budget plan. I wrote everything down and budgeted for £25 a week. It hasn't worked very well, but the first term is harder though. There's this compulsion to spend." (female first year)

> "No, not at all. You know how much you've got, and you know you want to spend it so you've got just enough at the end of term so as not to go into the overdraft. I have a vague idea of a limit – I wouldn't just spend aimlessly." (male final year)

Some patterns did emerge, however, and it was possible to group the different strategies mentioned by students into four provisional 'styles' of money management. Quotes typifying the four main styles of money management are outlined below:

> **The non-budgeter**: "I don't make any budget plans and don't really worry about my money. I just spend money as and when I need to, or when I feel like it, and this hasn't caused many problems in the past. I don't keep a careful track on how much I'm spending, but I'd know if there was a problem, and I know I could do something about it."

> **The retro-budgeter**: "I don't really make very strict budget plans. I write down how much money I've taken out of my account, what cheques I've written, any payments I've made with my card, and roughly what I've spent it all on, just so that I know where it's all going. If I've had a really expensive week, I might try and cut down a bit the following week."

> **The semi-budgeter**: "I know how much money I have available to me each term, and how much is left per week, after paying for my accommodation. This is only a rough guideline, however, and I don't mind spending over the limit a bit. Some weeks will always be more expensive than others, and there is always the overdraft to fall back on."

> **The budgeter**: "I know exactly how much money I have available to me each term, and I work out how much I'll have left each week, after paying for my accommodation. I might also put aside set amounts to pay for my books and travel, and other large expenses, just so that I know I've got enough to last me through the term. I try as much as possible to stick to my weekly limit."

Very few participants categorised themselves as a 'budgeter' during the second phase of the study, so the 'budgeter' and 'semi-budgeter' categories were combined for further analysis. Table 2.1 shows the frequencies for the three remaining money management style groups.

It can be seen in Table 2.1 that men were more likely to be non-budgeters than women (25/13), and that women were more likely to be semi-budgeters than men (21/6). It was also found that participants who saw their income as fixed were more likely to be semi-budgeters (22) than those who did not (5). Although there were no significant associations between year of study and money management style it is noteworthy that all five of those who originally categorised themselves as 'budgeters' according to the provisional styles of money management outlined above were first year students.

The majority of participants stated that 'managing with what you have got' most represented successful money management (63%), and 'staying out of debt' represented the second most popular response (21%). Only a minority of participants chose alternative categories: 'having fun, no matter what the cost', 'spending now, worrying about it later', and 'getting by on as little as possible so that you can save for the future'.

Table 2.1: Breakdown of the sample according to gender, perception of income, year of study and money management style

	n	Non-budgeter	Retro-budgeter	Semi-budgeter
Men	42	25	11	6
Women	48	13	14	21
Fixed income	54	17	15	22
Non-fixed income	46	21	10	5
First years	46	17	13	16
Final years	44	21	12	11
All participants	90	38	25	27

Multiple regression was conducted in an attempt to predict money management style from 13 items included in the questionnaire[6]. With other variables held constant, it was found that stricter money management styles were associated with perceiving income as fixed, being female, having a student loan, credit card use, and intolerant attitudes towards credit and debt. A negative association was also found between budgeting and 'asset holdings', with those participants stating that personal assets formed a large part of their income being less likely to be semi-budgeters.

Spending preferences

A section of questions examined whether, for those students not using fixed budget plans, there were certain items that were underconsumed, or for which the amount of money spent was limited. For nearly all of the participants, 'luxury items' such as clothes and music were considered unnecessary expenditures, whereas (for the majority) food and alcohol were almost always allowed, regardless of the cost. This finding that expenditures on certain goods and services were limited, while others continued to be purchased even when the individual's financial situation was dire, suggests that preferences that might not be anticipated from a purely rational model of financial decision making, play a central role.

Similar patterns of frequencies were found across all of the subsamples, but certain differences were found between first years and finalists, and between men and women. For example, men included alcohol as a main category more than women (23/9), and women incorporated clothes more often than men (18/13). First years included clothes more than finalists did (20/11), who referred to going out more frequently (35/25).

The main categories of items limited by all participants are shown in Figure 2.3. Perhaps the most striking feature of Figure 2.3 is that only 15 participants indicated that they would limit expenditure on alcohol (few more than would cut down on food consumption), yet 58 participants would cut down on outgoings for clothes. Another point of interest is that women were more likely to limit their spending on all categories more than men (for example, clothes 38/20, going out 22/16).

Figure 2.4 presents the categories of items which participants stated they always bought regardless of their financial situation at the time. It is reassuring to note that the most common 'unlimited' expenditure

Figure 2.3: Categories of items for which expenditure was limited

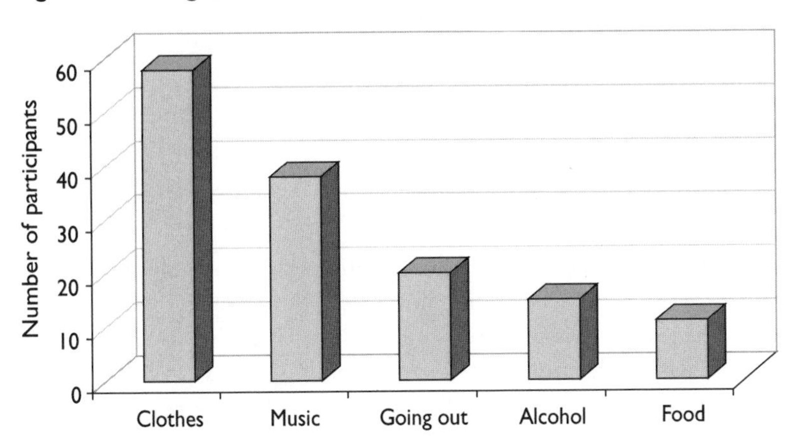

Figure 2.4: Categories of items for which expenditure was 'unlimited'

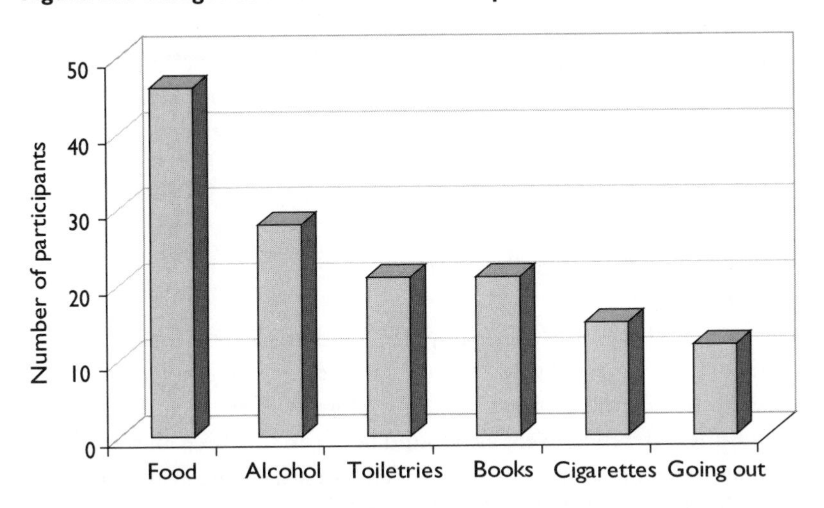

category was food, with 46 participants stating that they would not limit their spending regardless of their financial position. A little less heartening, however, was the finding that more participants believed alcohol should always be purchased (28) than toiletries (21).

There were also a few subsample differences worth mentioning. Slightly more first year than final year students included alcohol and going out in their unlimited spending group (17 and 11/11 and 5), and more final year students included the staple category of food (27/19). Overall, fewer women than men specified unlimited categories, although higher frequencies for the categories of toiletries (17/4) and cigarettes (22/4) were obtained compared to men.

Study 3

Spending limits

The final study reported on in this chapter set out to establish whether students set themselves spending limits and, if so, to see if they were able to stick to them. Students self-reported on their method of keeping track of how much money they were spending, as shown in Table 2.2. As can be seen, the majority (68%) thought they had a reasonable idea of the amount they were spending, but only 23% actually claimed to keep a full written record. In terms of spending limits, intention did not match reality. Only 39% of participants were able to keep to their weekly spending limits (of the 60% who actually set them in the first place), and as few as 35% claimed to set and keep to a spending limit on a 'good' night out. Having said this, 74% of participants claimed to try to reduce their spending following an expensive week, but this does not mean that they actually succeeded.

Styles of money management

Hierarchical cluster analysis was performed to search for groups of participants who tended to answer the questions in similar ways, and three homogeneous groups of cases, or 'clusters', were identified. Some interesting differences were also found between the three clusters when *nominal logistic regression* was conducted to predict group membership from the items included in the questionnaire[7].

Table 2.2: Participants' self-reported method of keeping track of spending

Method of tracking expenditure	%
"I don't really keep track of what I'm spending"	9
"I only have a rough mental idea about what I'm spending"	34
"I keep track mentally of what I'm spending and budget mentally"	34
"I am fully aware of how much I'm spending and budget carefully on paper"	23

- **Cluster 1** contained 22 participants who were fairly conservative spenders and reasonably aware of their expenditure. They tended to keep to spending limits when socialising and avoided the use of credit cards, which suggests they were in control of their spending and not prone to the excesses associated with the two clusters that follow. They were also likely to have more than one bank account, which appears, in consideration of the other factors, to signify the effective organisation of finances.
- **Cluster 2** included 54 participants, and arguably represented the 'typical' student, who were reasonably controlled when it came to budgeting even if they were not very conservative spenders: 93% possessed a credit card. They had a rough idea of their weekly expenditure and set themselves a weekly spending limit, but did not worry too much if they failed to keep to it.
- **Cluster 3** consisted of 21 participants, representing the group that was least careful with money. They were not careful with their finances, nor were they fully aware of how much they were spending. Their situation was made worse by their proneness to excessive spending and their lack of limiting expenditure following an expensive week. It was interesting to note, however, that like the students from cluster one, they avoided the use of credit cards.

Discussion will now turn to the common themes that run through all three of these studies, despite their being conducted independently.

Summary and theoretical implications

The majority of students described good money management as 'managing with what you have got', which is likely to reflect the inability of most to avoid some form of borrowing. A large proportion of students had more than one bank account, not just their student account, and they assigned different sources of income and distinct categories of expenditure to these separate accounts.

Men tended to spend more than women, particularly on alcohol, and were poor at cutting back on social expenditures. Women, by comparison, were better able to prioritise their expenditures and were more inclined to adopt some form of budgeting system. Despite these gender differences, students of both sexes failed to manage their money with any great care or foresight, often choosing to live well above their means, especially in terms of social expenditure and alcohol consumption.

Although there was some evidence to suggest that certain expenditures were limited during times of financial hardship, most continued to consume alcohol no matter what.

A possible explanation for this willingness of students to borrow comparatively more than other low-income groups in the general population is offered by the life-cycle hypothesis (LCH) pioneered by Modigliani and Brumberg (1954). According to the LCH students are behaving rationally, borrowing during a temporary period of low income that will be more than compensated for by their future earnings. Similarly, according to the LCH it is rational for men to borrow more than women, because their lifetime earnings are likely to be greater.

If this is the case, however, why is it that participants tried to organise their finances into different accounts and attempted to limit certain expenditures? It is also important to note that money management styles were related to perceptions of current income, with those viewing their finances as fixed being more likely to budget. This suggests that, rather than being rational, students are somewhat short-sighted in terms of their expenditure, which is more in keeping with the behavioural life-cycle hypothesis (BLCH) proposed by Shefrin and Thaler (1988).

Notes

[1] More detailed information concerning the research methods is included in Appendix A.

[2] All statistical analysis techniques written in *italics* are included in the glossary (Appendix B).

[3] Quotes from the qualitative phases of research have been used to illustrate the quantitative results where appropriate.

[4] A feature of the government loan scheme at this time was its availability to all students, including the better off who were not previously in receipt of grants.

[5] The mean scaled question scores for men and women are included in Table C1 (Appendix C).

[6] The results of the *multiple regression* to predict money management style are included in Table C2 (Appendix C).

[7] Results of the *nominal logistic regressions* to differentiate the three clusters are included in Table C3 (Appendix C).

THREE

Student debt: expecting it, spending it and regretting it

Stephen E.G. Lea, Paul Webley and Guy Bellamy

Introduction

This chapter aims to expand on the approach of Davies and Lea (1995) by devising a comprehensive model of student debt using quantitative research methods including *principal component analysis* and *regression analysis*. The work of Davies and Lea has been further developed in three ways. First, samples were not only drawn from current students but also from prospective students (students in the penultimate year of the school system, preparing to apply for university places) and former students (recent graduates). Second, a much larger and more representative sample of current students was used, allowing more detailed analysis. Finally, as well as measuring attitudes towards credit and debt, two other psychological issues, linked to borrowing by Morgan, Roberts and Powdrill in Chapter Two, were included: spending patterns and money management. Spending patterns are significant as it is likely that financial problems are linked to particular forms of consumer behaviour, and interview studies have found at least some evidence to support this idea (for example, Walker, 1997; Walker et al, 1992). Similarly, money management is important because interviews and subsequent survey research on general population samples have shown strong associations between levels of debt and people's self-reports of their ability to plan their finances, even with variations in economic circumstances taken into account (for example, Lea et al, 1995).

In light of the previous literature, an outline scheme of the relationship between financial behaviour and psychological variables can be proposed; it is sketched in Figure 3.1. The present research aims both to test this model and to fill in some of the detail which it lacks.

Figure 3.1: Conceptual model of the origins of student financial behaviour and attitudes

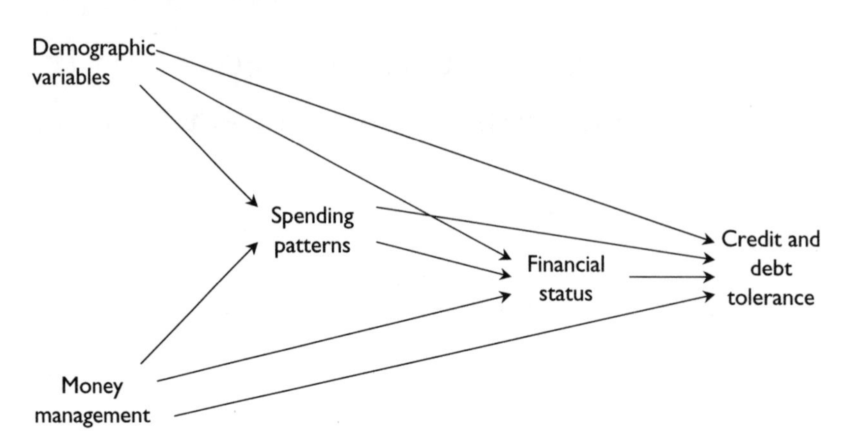

The samples and the questionnaires[1]

The questionnaires were distributed to three groups: prospective students, current students, and former students.

The prospective student sample consisted of 659 16- and 17-year-old pupils in the first year of the 'sixth form' (Year 12) at schools or attending further education colleges in Devon. The current student sample consisted of 1,129 students taking degree courses at the University of Exeter, of which 38% were classified as first years, 29% as mid-course, and 23% as finalists. The 10% who were postgraduates were treated as a separate group. Finally, the former student sample consisted of 54 recent graduates of the University of Exeter with addresses in the UK.

Different questionnaires were used for the three samples. All started with simple demographic details (age, gender, parents' occupations), and all ended with the 14 item scale of attitudes towards credit and debt used by Davies and Lea (1995)[2]. The central part of the prospective student questionnaire included questions about participants' estimates of a student's financial needs, sources of financial support and expenditure, and about their present financial situation. The central part of the current student questionnaire asked about their present financial situation (average bank balance and greatest borrowing in the current academic year), their sources of income, their typical expenditure, their financial and employment expectations on leaving university, and their experience with their bank. The central part of the former student questionnaire asked about the participants' financial situation when they were students, their views on the causes and consequences of their own and others' financial difficulties when they were students, and their employment and financial experience since graduating.

Results[3]

Experience of student debt

Within the current student sample, some experience of borrowing was common. Most students reported average bank balances in the range of £400 overdrawn to £400 credited to their account. Among first-years, only 16% reported averages below zero, but this figure rose to 33% with mid-course students and 45% with finalists. The number who reported no borrowing at any point of the year fell from 33% for first years to 10% for final year undergraduates[4]. Across years, 38% reported having a government student loan (slightly lower than the national figure of 44%), but only 5% mentioned such loans when asked to describe their 'debt position'. This suggests that such long-term arranged borrowings are not recognised as 'debt' by current students. The former students, on the other hand, typically included student loans among what they described as their 'debts'.

The limits to economic socialisation: anticipating future economic circumstances

All three samples were asked about their current economic circumstances, and the prospective students and current university students were asked some questions about what they thought their financial position would be when they reached the next stage. They revealed some significant misapprehensions.

School pupils were reasonably accurate about the amount of money undergraduates typically spent – 62% of them estimated between £3,000 and £6,000 per year, and 62% of undergraduates estimated their expenditure as lying within this bracket. But when compared with the undergraduates' reports, school pupils underestimated the proportion of undergraduate expenditure which goes on what can be called 'discretionary' items – alcohol, cigarettes, clubbing, music, presents, holidays, car and petrol costs[5]. The undergraduate sample reported that these discretionary categories accounted for 30% of all expenditure, while the prospective students expected the figure to be 12%.

Undergraduates, on the other hand, tended to overestimate their future spending power. A typical starting salary for a 1994 graduate would be around £13,000 per annum, from which it would be reasonable to expect a new graduate to retain about £200 per month as discretionary income, yet 75% of the current student sample expected their discretionary income to be higher than this; 43% expected it to be higher than £400 per month.

Cross-sample comparison of attitudes towards credit and debt

Figure 3.2 shows the mean level of tolerance towards credit and debt recorded in the three samples, with the current student sample broken down into the four study groups[6].

Two trends are obvious. First, as in the results of Davies and Lea's study (1995), mean responses are slightly on the side of tolerance: mean scores all lie between 4 and 5, where a score of 5 corresponds to an answer of 'slightly disagree' to an item expressing disapproval of credit and debt, and 4 is the point of 'no opinion'. Second, there is a strong non-monotonic trend, which represents a bell-shaped curve, with school pupils showing the lowest levels of tolerance towards credit and debt, final year undergraduates the highest, and postgraduate student and graduate groups showing a return to mean levels more like those of school pupils. Although there were sharp differences in the financial situations of the prospective, current and former student samples, these could not be due to any attitude differences, so the large differences

Figure 3.2: Mean credit and debt tolerance scores for school, university and ex-students

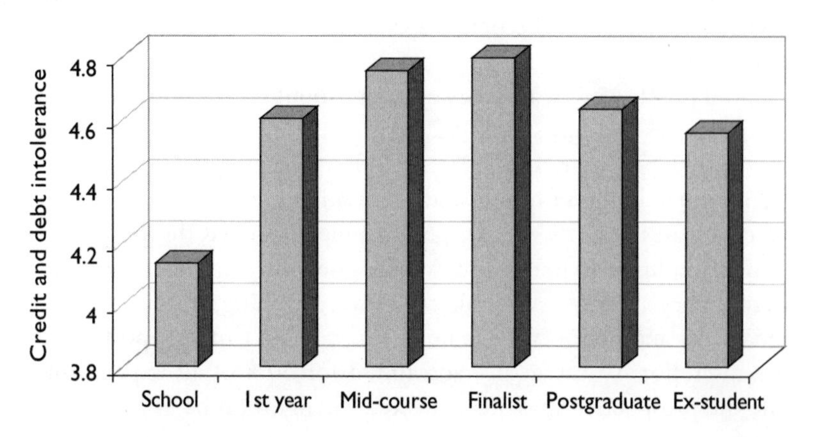

seen between the three main samples in Figure 3.2 must be consequences of the financial circumstances. It is reasonable to suppose that the differences between stages of study in the current student group have a similar explanation.

Exogenous variables in the analysis of the current student group

Further analysis concentrated on the current student group, for which the most detailed data were available. Data from 565 respondents were used, comprising those for whom complete information on all the variables shown in Figure 3.1 was available.

Following the logic of Figure 3.1, demographic variables and money management were taken as external variables. The demographic variables used were gender, age group, stage of study, socio-economic class and credit card use[7]. As regards age, respondents were classified as teenagers, early 20s or over 25s. Social class was assessed from parents' occupations, and money management was assessed by students' self-reports of their ability to plan their finances.

Determination of spending patterns

The variables influencing spending patterns were the first to be considered. Students were asked to estimate their monthly expenditure on the following 18 categories: alcohol, car, books, music, holidays, buying presents, clubbing, public transport, clubs and societies, toiletries, rent and bills (for example, utilities), petrol, sport, clothes, cigarettes, council tax, food and 'other'. To make the data more suitable for statistical treatment, they were first reduced to categories of £0/month, £1-£5/ month, and so on up to £46-£50/month; thereafter £10 categories were used, with a maximum score being given to reported expenditures of over £100/month. This category system captured the credible detail of all types of expenditure well, except for rent and bills where the amounts were higher; in this case categories of £0, £1-£25, £26-£50 and so on were used, with a maximum score for reported expenditures of over £300/month.

The transformed spending scores were then submitted to *principal component analysis* to seek out a set of independent 'factors', each representing a different type of spending. Six factors were obtained, all of which have been given at least a provisional interpretation. For example, spending on books, music, presents, toiletries and clothes were all positively loaded on Factor 1. Factor 2 had positive loadings on car and petrol costs, and a negative loading on public transport. Factor 3 was positive on alcohol, clubbing and cigarettes; 4 on rent, bills and food; 5 on clubs, societies and sport; and finally 6 on holidays and other expenditures. Factors 1 and 3 are particularly interesting. Factor 1, spending on personal items, seems to correspond to the sort of personal spending that is likely to be typical of any young individual, while Factor 3, spending on socialising, represents the spending of the stereotypical student socialite – alcohol, cigarettes, and clubbing. Scores on these six factors were used for all subsequent analysis of spending patterns shown in Table 3.1.

Table 3.1: Multiple regressions to predict the six spending factors from demographic variables and ability to plan

Factors and their interpretations	**1**	**2**	**3**	**4**	**5**	**6**
	Personal	**Car**	**Socialising**	**House**	**Sport**	**Holidays etc**
Effects of exogenous variables						
Male gender	–***	+***	+***			+***
Higher socio-economic class			+**			
Credit card use	+*	+***				
Age group						
teens		–**		–***		
over 25		+***	–**			–*
Stage of study						
1st year				–***		
finalist		+*				
postgraduate			–*			–***
Ability to plan financially			–***			
R^2_{adj}	2.9%	15.8%	5.7%	28.2%	0%	5.3%
$F_{8,556}$	3.12**	14.22***	5.28***	28.69***	0.98	4.97***

Notes: + signs indicate positive loadings on the factor, – negative loadings; asterisks indicate significant effects in multiple regression (* $p<.05$, ** $p<.01$, *** $p<.001$).

Linear regression was then used to predict each of the six spending factors from the exogenous variables. Although goodness of fit was poor for all factors, the data were sufficient to show that spending patterns related to both demographic variables and ability to plan, but that different variables affected different factors. Most of the relationships observed are readily interpretable. In particular, Factors 2 and 4, associated with car ownership and occupancy of a house or other self-catering accommodation, were higher among the over 25s and lower among teenagers and (for Factor 4) first year undergraduates; while Factor 3, spending on socialising, was higher among males and those of higher socio-economic class, and lower among mature students.

Correlates of financial position

Next, an attempt was made to predict respondents' financial status from demographic variables, ability to plan financially, and spending patterns. Examination of the responses to questions about students' current financial position showed that there were four common situations, defined as follows:

- **Permanent debt** These students, 33% of the sample, reported owing money all or most of the time, with negative average bank balances.
- **Fluctuating debt** These students, 33% of the sample, reported bank balances that averaged in credit, but acknowledged some borrowing at times during the academic year.
- **Non-debtors** Most of the remaining sample (27%) reported that they did not owe money at any point in the academic year.
- **Credit users** This relatively small group, 6% of the sample, reported high credit balances but also the highest levels of 'maximum' debt.

The first three of the above groups fall into an ordered sequence of financial health, but it is not obvious how the final group should be assimilated to this sequence. They are reminiscent of Katona's (1975) observation that in a general public sample the highest levels of borrowing are found in consumers with the highest income, because they can afford to use large amounts of credit. Credit use among this group of students is clearly a distinct kind of phenomenon, and they were excluded from the quantitative analyses which follow; for consistency, they were also excluded from the analyses of the determination of spending patterns reported above.

Ordered logit regression was used to best predict financial status from three groups of independent variables – demographic, planning, and spending factors. When each group of variables was taken on its own, financial status was found to be significantly better in teenagers, females, first years, and those who reported they could plan their finances; it was worse among finalists and among those with high scores on the spending factors associated with car use, socialising, and living in a house or other self-catering accommodation. When all variables were considered together, independently significant effects were found only for ability to plan, being a finalist, and having a high score on the spending on socialising factor (Factor 3).

Predicting attitudes towards credit and debt

Finally, the demographic variables, planning, spending patterns and financial status were all used to predict scores on the scale of attitudes towards credit and debt. Again the four sets of variables were used in all combinations. Variables from all groups were significantly associated with attitudes when each group was used on its own: less tolerant attitudes towards credit and debt were shown by teenagers, those who could plan their finances, those in a good financial position, and those with lower scores on spending Factors 3, 4, and 5, associated respectively with socialising, house/self-catering accommodation, and sport. Demographic variables, however, did not significantly improve the prediction of attitudes from the other variables. *Stepwise regression* was used to find the combination of individual variables that most efficiently predicted attitudes towards credit and debt; a model including financial status, ability to plan financially, and the three spending factors was identified.

A detailed model of borrowing and attitudes towards credit and debt

The need to use *ordered logit regression* to predict the categorical variable of financial status meant that a formal *path analysis* could not be used to integrate the relationships between variables discussed above. The results can be put together informally, however, to suggest an expanded version of Figure 3.1, and this is shown in Figure 3.3. Only effects that were significant in *multivariate analyses* (analyses involving more than one dependent variable) are included.

Figure 3.3: Elaborated model of the origins of student financial behaviour and attitudes

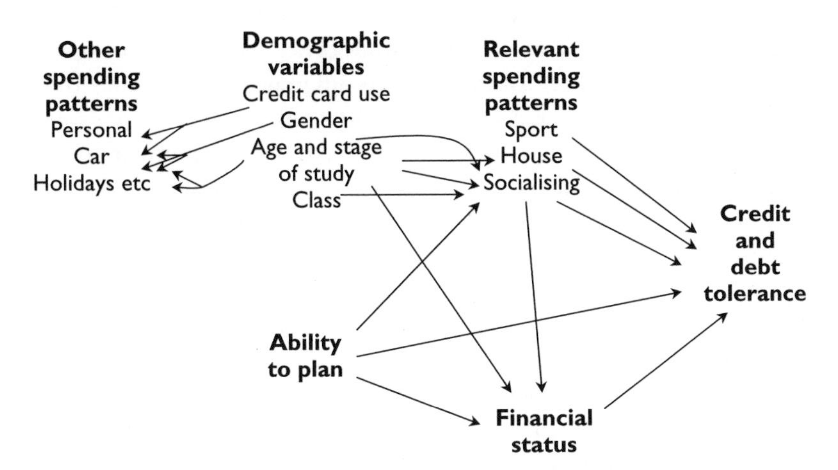

A model of student debt

Figure 3.3 provides a convenient starting point for the discussion of the results. It is an extended version of Figure 3.1, with details added wherever possible.

First, some points of uncertainty in the analysis. It could be argued that the ability to plan one's finances, and also credit card use, are consequences rather than causes of spending patterns or financial state. The decision to treat them as exogenous variables was based partly on discussions with current students. These were informal, and additional longitudinal research is needed to test the impression that the ability to plan one's finances and credit card use tend to be stable, long-term aspects of financial behaviour, at least compared with the timescale of a university career. Obviously, the age group and stage of study variables are strongly correlated (though a minority of mature students are found at every stage of study); but it was duly found that the two variables had almost identical effects. Most importantly, only showing the results that were significant in the *multivariate analyses* means that the model is a little 'bare': there are certainly additional, perhaps smaller effects that could be revealed by further analysis or research.

Second, what do these results say about the question of student debt and attitudes towards credit and debt? The present study comes as close as any cross-sectional study can to settling the question of the relationship between attitudes and behaviour in the matter of student debt. The variations in financial circumstances between school pupils, current university students, and recent graduates are objective and it cannot plausibly be argued that they are due to varying attitudes in the different samples. The substantial disparities in attitudes between the three groups must be the consequence of these group differences. The results thus confirm the conclusions reached, much more tentatively, by Davies and Lea (1995): the experience of credit use, which is a common feature of student life, helps induce a more tolerant attitude towards credit and debt. It is also notable that no direct effects of demographic variables on the attitude score were found: the results suggest that such effects are indirect consequences of demographic differences in spending behaviour and consequent financial status. Of course, the different sampling techniques used mean that the three groups do differ in non-financial ways, most obviously in age. But the onus must be on anyone who wants to argue that these differences, rather than economic circumstances, produce different attitudes towards credit and debt to demonstrate how that comes about.

Finally, what does cause students to borrow? As other studies have shown, it appears that the first and most obvious reason is lack of money (for example, Lea et al, 1993, 1995). Full-time study does not allow full-time earning, and in the absence of government grants the cost of living away from home is sufficient to ensure that most students will rely on loans to some extent. It is clear, however, that individual differences have a sharp influence on the outcome. As in both interview and survey studies of poor people in the general population, it seems that money management is a critically important factor (for example, Walker, 1997; Lea et al, 1995). The relative homogeneity of the student group allows other factors to be seen more clearly as well. Spending patterns, in particular spending on socialising (alcohol, cigarettes and clubbing), have a significant effect, and these in turn reflect demographic variables. Few people who have much to do with UK undergraduates will be surprised to learn that men, and those from higher socio-economic classes, are likely to spend more on these kinds of expenditures, and are correspondingly more likely to end up owing money, while mature students show the opposite pattern.

The influence of 'social' spending on credit use should be linked to the results of the investigation of prospective students' knowledge of the financial situation they would face as undergraduates. Recall that school pupils underestimated the proportion of undergraduate expenditure that goes on discretionary items. From one point of view, they were underestimating the discretionary spending power they would experience as undergraduates. From another, they were underestimating the social necessity of what might be looked on as luxury consumption. It would be easy for parents and others trying to help school pupils prepare for university life to be censorious about this kind of expenditure, but it might be more appropriate to prepare them for it. After all, the variable most consistent in predicting financial health is the ability to plan expenditure, and accurate planning is more likely to be possible if you know what your likely expenditures will be, rather than what someone else thinks it ought to be.

Notes

[1] More detailed information concerning the research methods is included in Appendix A.

[2] Davies and Lea's (1995) 14 attitude statements are given in Appendix D.

[3] All statistical analysis techniques written in *italics* are included in the glossary (Appendix B).

[4] A validity check was carried out on the current students' reports of their financial circumstances. The average bank balances reported by the 57% of the sample who said they held an account with the National Westminster Bank were calculated. These figures were then compared with the bank's statistics on mean bank balances for student customers in the same period. The two figures agreed within 3%.

[5] Such spending is not quite what Katona (1975) described as discretionary expenditure because he emphasised that this should not include habitual purchasing, whereas quite a lot of these items would be bought on a regular basis. But it is the closest available term.

[6] The reliability of the attitude scale was tested using the current student sample and was found to be reasonably satisfactory (*Cronbach's alpha* of 0.70) based on the 989 respondents who answered all 14 attitude questions.

[7] Both age and stage of study were observed to enter into some non-monotonic relationships, so they were replaced by *dummy variables* (categorical independent variables).

FOUR

Student loans: the development of a new dependency culture?

Adrian J. Scott and Alan Lewis

Introduction

The aim of this chapter is to look at levels of debt at both the time of graduation and 16 months later, thus continuing the story of student debt, as told in Chapters Two and Three, into the postgraduation future. Unlike the research in the previous chapters, however, this study has a longitudinal aspect, as the same respondents were asked to tell us about their borrowing behaviour at the two points in time. Hence the study has a better chance of unravelling the causes of graduate debt. In particular, this chapter explores the relationship between student loan use and gender, and the longer-term formation of more tolerant attitudes towards credit and debt.

A closer examination of the student loan scheme, as a form of borrowing, is of particular interest because of the reasoning behind its introduction: to tackle the financial shortfalls of the grant system. As Leonard (1995) pointed out, however, changes in the financing of higher education were not only driven by financial considerations but also by the belief among policy makers that students were becoming part of a 'dependency culture', a dependency that could be broken by the loan scheme. Leonard quoted John McGregor, the then Secretary of State: "... top-up loans will secure changes in student attitudes, [will diminish their] dependency on the state [and] will promote a proper sense of reliance and responsibility" (Hansard, 1989, cited in Leonard, 1995).

Research into the impact of the loan scheme also has practical importance as studies on student debt suggest that an attitudinal acceptability of credit and debt develops during an undergraduate's career (Davies and Lea, 1995; Lea, Webley and Bellamy, Chapter Three); that students have a more tolerant attitude towards credit and debt than the rest of the population (Lea et al, 1993); and that tolerant attitudes towards credit and debt correlate with the amount a person is willing to borrow in the future (Livingstone and Lunt, 1992). If, therefore, individuals continue to have tolerant attitudes towards credit and debt after graduation, having been socialised to accept credit use, they might be more likely to borrow in the future and experience problems with repayments should unforeseen adverse economic circumstances arise (Davies and Lea, 1995).

The sample and the questionnaire[1]

One hundred and eighty-eight recent graduates of the University of Bath took part in the questionnaire study: 81 were male (43%) and 107 were female (57%). The mean age of participants was 23; mature students were excluded from the sample because of their varied financial and domestic circumstances.

Similar to Lea, Webley and Bellamy's research (Chapter Three), the questionnaire started with simple demographic details (age, gender) and ended with the 14 item scale of student attitudes towards student debt developed by Davies and Lea three years before their 1995 publication. The central part of the questionnaire asked about participants' levels of debt at the time of graduation and at the time of the survey, and more specifically, how much they owed to each of the following: bank overdrafts, student loans, credit cards, family and friends, and 'other'. Participants were also asked if they were currently employed and whether their gross annual income was more or less than the threshold figure below which student loan repayments could be deferred, at the time £1,374 a month (DfEE, 1998).

Results and discussion[2]

This section starts with the reported level and form of borrowings, both at the time of graduation and 16 months later, highlighting any sex differences. This is followed by the results from the attitude items and the calculation of a single 'acceptability of credit and debt' score. This score is then used to assess whether there are any differences between the sexes, those in debt and those without debt. A *multiple regression* follows to assess whether being in debt in general, or more specifically borrowing through the student loan scheme, has the greatest influence on students' acceptability of credit and debt; gender was also included in this analysis. Finally an attempt is made to unravel the interactions between gender, credit use, and the acceptability of credit and debt, and to consider the question of the likely effects of the kind of economic socialisation encountered during undergraduate study[3].

At the time of graduation 78% of participants were in debt, with average borrowings of £4,222. At the time of the survey (16 months later) 70% of participants were in debt, with average borrowings of £4,388. By comparing these figures with those of previous research it is evident that there has been an increase in the use of credit as well as the level of debt – when Davies and Lea (1995) conducted their research in 1992, they found that 67% of final year students had some debt, with average borrowings of £814. The combination of these findings and the following participant comments suggest that credit use is increasingly considered to be an inevitable part of university life:

> "With so little grant money I had to borrow in order to survive." (female, 24)

> "With ever increasing costs for accommodation, food, fees ... it is hardly surprising that we all end up in debt." (female, 23)

> "It is very difficult not to get into debt as a student." (female, 24)

Having commented on the apparent inevitability of credit use, however, it is worth mentioning that some other participants acknowledged the importance of spending patterns and poor money management as possible causes of high levels of debt. Examples include:

> "... equally as many [students] blow their student loans on alcohol and unnecessary items. Saving as a student can be very hard, equally however it can be fairly easy." (female, 23)

> "... many of my friends who complained of low grants, lack of money, access funds, etc, were the worst money managers I have ever met, spending far more money on beer than food, rent or books. Prioritisation is not something instilled in student life! The easy availability of student loans and interest-free overdrafts does little to dispel the belief that this is anything other than 'easy money'. The first thing students do with their loan is spend, spend, spend." (male, 23)

> "If students can afford to drink beer every night, they are not poor. Many students I knew complained of poverty, and yet were 'wasted' every evening." (male, 23)

Another important finding was that there had been little change in levels of debt over the 16-month time period. The majority of graduates continued to have large borrowings, with only a few individuals (10%) having been able to clear their student debt. The lack of repayment over the 16 months suggests that student borrowings are no longer relatively small in comparison to graduate incomes, as they were in 1992 when Davies and Lea conducted their research, but instead continue to hinder individuals for several years after graduation. This outcome also took a number of participants by surprise, as the following quotes illustrate:

> "When I took out my student loan I didn't really think about the repayments. I now have to make repayments every month for five years, which affects the amount you can borrow for a mortgage." (female, 23)

> "Banks and other lending institutions such as the government are not making it clear to students how difficult it is after university to pay back large sums of money. They encourage short-term drinking ... instead of long-term [planning].... If students were more aware of these factors they might be somewhat more careful when borrowing money." (female, 23)

> "From a personal point of view, if I had known how much a degree in psychology was going to cost me over the four years I would never have done it. I have also found it to be of little use in finding a job, so in order to earn enough money for a reasonable standard of living and pay off my loans, I have had to pay to do further 'vocational' training. On the whole I wish I had gone straight to work from school and had sponsorship by the company for vocational training – saving a lot of wasted time and money." (female, 25)

These participant comments imply that a proportion of graduates did not truly understand the full extent of their borrowings until repayments began. Instead, they took on high levels of debt while at university without considering the long-term consequences of their actions. This is reminiscent of the behavioural life-cycle hypothesis proposed by

Shefrin and Thaler (1988). It should also be noted that Seaward and Kemp (2000) refer to an 'underlying optimistic disposition' in their New Zealand student sample, who believed their borrowings would be repaid far sooner than the government statistics concerning student loan repayment indicated.

Having looked at changes in the use and level of debt between graduation and the time of the survey, differences in the forms of borrowing were considered. Figure 4.1 shows the relative use of different forms of borrowing at the time of graduation and 16 months later.

The figure highlights two areas of interest: the decreasing use of bank overdrafts and the increasing use of other loans. Although bank overdrafts were the most frequently used form of borrowing at the time of graduation, the number of participants using them had halved 16 months later. Over the same time period, the number of participants using other loans, the majority of which were graduate loans, showed a large (proportional) increase. The changing use of different forms of borrowing may reflect changes in opportunity and need as well as changes in interest rates. For example, the decreasing use of bank overdrafts probably reflects participants' efforts to repay their interest-free overdrafts prior to the introduction of interest rates a year after graduation. The rise in the use of other loans by comparison is probably the result of their increased availability: graduates are frequently targeted by loan packages that aim to 'help them get started'. Having exhausted their student loans and overdraft(s), other loans provide a new source of finance. It is also

Figure 4.1: Forms of borrowing at the time of graduation and 16 months later

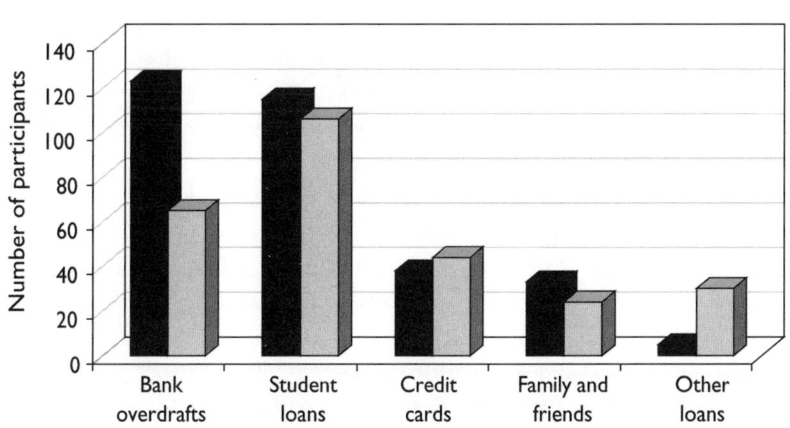

notable that the use of 'other loans' 16 months after graduation was associated with previous credit use, with 29 of the 30 participants having had some form of borrowing on graduation. *Chi-square analysis* found that the relationship between the use of other loans and previous credit use was statistically significant, $\chi^2=7.15, p<.01$.

The acceptability of credit and debt

Factor analysis was used to uncover the underlying structure of the attitude scale and discovered that seven of the original 14 items designed by Davies and Lea (1995) were loaded on a single factor (that is, were highly intercorrelated), explaining 27% of the variance[4]. The mean scores and standard deviations are presented in Table 4.1. This factor had a satisfactory reliability score, *Cronbach's alpha* of 0.74, and has been labelled the 'acceptability of credit and debt' measure[5]. In subsequent analysis a summation of these items into a single score is used (with the appropriate raw data reversals); the other items are not reported because, with this graduate sample, they reduced the reliability of the scale. Items answered by a sample of school pupils (n=179), mainly aged 17 and 18, in their final two years at a West of England comprehensive coeducational school, have also been included for comparison (Lewis and Scott, 1999).

The table shows a tolerance among graduates towards credit and debt but it needs to be put into context. *Independent samples t-tests* were conducted to compare the average item scores of 17- and 18-year-old school pupils with those of graduates (the largest differences were for items 2, 3 and 5). The analysis showed that graduates are less keen on saving before making purchases, $t=8.29, p<.001$, are more likely to agree loans are a good thing, $t=-6.50, p<.001$, and are less likely to agree that borrowing money is wrong, $t=6.66, p<.001$. These results are consistent with the means for the full 14 item Davies and Lea scale reported by Lea, Webley and Bellamy in Chapter Three.

On graduation males had, on average, borrowings of £3,923 and females £2,830; 16 months later these differences were £3,569 and £2,712 respectively[6]. Thus the men had made a bigger dent in their student debt than the women. The difference in the amount paid off is small, however, and there is still a substantial gender difference in levels of debt 16 months after graduation, though it falls just short of statistical significance ($t=1.82$, $p=.07$). A possible explanation for this finding relates to differences in income, as *chi-square analysis* showed that

Table 4.1: Mean acceptability of credit and debt scores for school pupils and graduates

Statements	School pupils (N=179) Mean (SD)	Graduates (N=188) Mean (SD)
1 It is better to have something now and pay for it later	3.5 (1.6)	3.2 (1.5)
2 You should always save up first before buying something	5.7 (1.1)***	4.5 (1.7)
3 Taking out a loan is a good thing because it allows you to enjoy (student) life	3.5 (1.4)***	4.5 (1.6)
4 You should always stay at home rather than borrow money to go out for an evening in the pub	n/a	4.5 (1.7)
5 Owing money is basically wrong	3.6 (1.2)***	2.6 (1.5)
6 There is no excuse for borrowing money	n/a	1.7 (0.8)
7 Banks should not give interest-free overdrafts to students	n/a	1.7 (1.1)

Notes: Attitude scores ranged from 'strongly disagree' (score 1) to 'strongly agree' (score 7); *** $p<.001$.

significantly more males (61%) than females (31%) had an annual income greater than £16,500, $\chi^2=16.48$, $p<.001$.

Two *independent samples t-tests* were calculated to see whether mean attitude scores differed according to gender and credit use. It was found that males had significantly higher acceptability of credit and debt scores than females, $t=2.35$, $p<.05$, a finding that agreed with those of previous research (for example, Davies and Lea, 1995; Lea, Webley and Bellamy, Chapter Three). Unfortunately it was impossible to find out the gender difference in attitudes at the time of graduation, but the finding that it was still significant while the difference in the levels of debt had begun to decline is consistent with the view of Davies and Lea (1995) and Lea, Webley and Bellamy, Chapter Three, that attitude change lags behaviour change. It does suggest, however, that attitudes might not be as quickly responsive to economic change as Lea and his colleagues have previously argued. Instead, it might be that students (and male students in particular) are socialised to see credit and debt as more acceptable and that this acceptability remains to a certain degree, even when the level of debt decreases. As Boddington and Kemp (1999) pointed out in relation to their New Zealand sample, there is no evidence that intolerance towards credit and debt ever returns to the level exhibited by school pupils.

Independent samples t-tests also revealed that participants in debt found credit and debt more acceptable than those without debt, t=4.85, p<.001, which again supported the findings of previous research (for example, Davies and Lea, 1995; Lea, Webley and Bellamy, Chapter Three). Having established that being in debt had an effect on the acceptability of credit and debt, a *Pearson product-moment correlation* was conducted to see whether the level of debt also had an effect. The output showed that the more a graduate owed (presumably up to a point!) the more acceptable credit and debt became, r=.20, p<.05. Although gender and credit use both had a significant relationship with attitudes towards credit and debt, the two variables were confounded since men are more likely to be in debt than women. Consequently, a *multiple linear regression* was used to look at the unique contributions of gender, student loans, and 'all other borrowings' in relation to attitudes towards credit and debt. The category 'all other borrowings' encompassed bank overdrafts, credit cards, family and friends, and other loans, and was used in the analysis because of their relative 'smallness' when compared to student loan borrowings[7].

The only independent variable to make a statistically significant unique contribution to predicting the acceptability of credit and debt was student loans (p<.001). This further supports Davies and Lea's proposal that attitudes towards credit and debt are primarily influenced by the use of credit: the lifestyles of male students lead to high levels of debt on graduation and it is this, rather than gender itself, that causes men to still have more tolerant attitudes towards credit and debt than women.

The strong effect of student loan use on the extent of postgraduation borrowing becomes of greater importance when the following participant comments are considered:

> "The only real debt I would allow myself from university is that of student loans due to the repayment conditions." (male, 23)

> "All loans should be based on student loans, whereby repayments are based on current income levels." (male, 23)

> "Taking out a student loan is a financial advantage as interest is linked to inflation, allowing one to enjoy time at university with the knowledge that the debt is not increasing in real terms, only inflationary." (male, 23)

> "The student loans are good because you don't have to repay them until you are earning. The interest levels are very low, so if you have

to borrow money, which as a student you do, they are the best option." (female, 23)

The above statements show that some graduates specifically chose student loans in preference to other types of borrowing while they were at university because of their relatively low interest rates and gradual repayment conditions, yet it was the only factor shown to have a significant effect on the acceptability of credit and debt, with participants who had a student loan viewing credit and debt as significantly more acceptable than those who did not. When related to Livingstone and Lunt's (1992) finding that tolerant attitudes towards credit and debt correlate with the amount a person is willing to borrow in the future, this result suggests that the student loan scheme might inadvertently lead to an increased propensity for graduates to take on new borrowings in the future.

Conclusion

Although the sample was a restricted one, the consistency of the results with previous studies suggests some tentative conclusions. The interrelationships between gender, credit use, and the acceptability of credit and debt are not straightforward. Women owed less, found credit and debt less acceptable, and were paying off student loans slightly less quickly. There is a gender effect on the acceptability of credit and debt, but it is not as strong as the effect of the loan scheme, and may be an indirect effect of the amount of borrowings accumulated.

There are good grounds for arguing that the student loan experience has a persistent effect. Student loans were still very much in evidence 16 months after graduation and are likely to continue to rise for future generations. Ultimately, does this matter? As the introduction to this chapter pointed out, one of the intentions of the loan scheme was that, as a process of economic socialisation, it would enhance economic knowledge, sophistication and responsibility. Taking this line of argument there is nothing to worry about; men are being rational and borrowing more because they know they can expect larger lifetime income from paid work in the future as predicted by the various life-cycle theories in economics (for example, Modigliani and Brumberg, 1954; Winnett and Lewis, 1995). The data reported in this chapter, however, favours a less optimistic interpretation. It suggests that the student loan scheme has not enhanced economic knowledge and responsibility, but legitimised borrowing from an early age, and that instead of breaking the dependency culture of reliance on the government it has simply transferred this dependency to form a new dependency on banks and financial institutions.

Notes

[1] More detailed information concerning the research methods is included in Appendix A.

[2] All statistical analysis techniques written in *italics* are included in the glossary (Appendix B).

[3] Participant comments included in the results were offered in response to a 'further comments' section of the questionnaire and illustrate the strength of feeling exhibited by some of the graduates.

[4] The *factor analysis* of the Davies and Lea's (1995) attitude scale is included in Table E1 (Appendix E).

[5] *Cronbach's alpha* tests the internal reliability of a set of items and for the purposes of research is considered internally consistent if the correlation coefficient is .70 or above (Hills, 1997).

[6] It is important to note that these averages and subsequent analysis include participants without debt.

[7] The results of the *multiple linear regression* to predict acceptability of credit and debt are included in Table E2 (Appendix E).

FIVE

The psychological effects of student debt

Steve Stradling

Introduction

The research presented in this chapter differs from the studies included in this book so far. Previous chapters have been primarily concerned with levels of debt and attitudes towards credit and debt; the current contribution deals instead with students' interpretations of their borrowings and the impact this has on their well-being. It has already been seen that students vary quite a lot in their financial behaviour, and it is likely that the impact borrowing has on them will also differ: as Hesketh (1999) argued, there may well be distinct types of student who respond differently to the prospect of being in debt.

As mentioned in previous chapters, the funding of higher education has moved from non-repayable subsidies to repayable student borrowings, with today's students mortgaging their futures against anticipated graduate-level earnings. Students have seen the disappearance of minimum maintenance grants, special equipment grants, eligibility for housing benefit in term time and for supplementary and unemployment benefits in vacation time, as well as the repeal of 'Fair Rents' legislation and the removal of income support.

In 1990 student loans were introduced and the proportion of students availing themselves of this facility has since increased inexorably, year after year. This has led some researchers to note, in the mid-1990s, that while "... students now have more money at their disposal ... much more of it is earned or borrowed against future earnings" (Callender and Kempson, 1996, p 17). University students have been moved from a 'gift culture', where the state invested directly in its future skilled manpower and educated citizenry, to a 'borrowing culture', where students (and their parents) invest against future earning power.

While those students not deterred by the anticipated costs of university may have sufficient financial resources to fund their years of study, what are the psychological effects of this change of culture on their interpretation of the situation and on the demands made on their personal, as opposed to their fiscal, resources? Three questionnaire studies investigating the psychological effects of student debt were conducted.

Method[1]

Study 1

In the first study, 612 prospective students who had been made conditional and unconditional offers by the University of Manchester took part. The questionnaire sought some demographic information (age, sex, courses and faculty applied for), anticipated levels of debt during and at the end of their undergraduate career, and self-rated levels of worry about their future indebtedness.

Study 2

In the second study, 223 final year undergraduate students, undertaking three- and four-year courses in Arts or Science subjects at the University of Manchester took part. Again, the questionnaire required some demographic details (age, sex, course and faculty) as well as information regarding their borrowing history, which sources of finance they used or anticipated using, ratings of their concern about financing their studies and the likelihood of a number of factors leading them to experience money troubles.

Study 3

In the third study, 99 undergraduate students, undertaking three- and four-year courses in Arts, Economic and Social Science, or Science and Engineering, at the University of Manchester took part. The questionnaire used in this study was very similar to that used in Study 2, only it requested the disclosure of the actual amounts received from each source of finance in the current academic year. It also included items concerning attitudes towards credit and debt, current financial difficulties, and present levels of anxiety and depression.

Results and discussion[2]

Results are reported from samples of 'mainstream' university students: direct entry (straight from school), male and female, predominantly Arts, Science and Social Science students, on three- and four-year honours programmes. While this chapter reports on levels of concern over graduating in debt, such figures should be extrapolated with caution to the body of UK higher education students. The concern here was not to establish population-wide figures, but rather to discern what other measures would best distinguish students who are worried, from those who are not.

Study 1

Of prospective students, 72% anticipated that they would end their student career in debt and 81% were concerned about financing their studies, with levels of concern significantly higher among female prospective students. When asked to estimate their likely levels of debt at the end of the first, second and third years of study most students estimated their likely figures as lower than the guide figures given (based on the average amount owed the previous year): the mean ratio of estimate to guide figure ranged from 0.67 for first year estimates to 0.80 for final year estimates. For each year, only about 15% of prospective students actually estimated their anticipated borrowings as being above the guide figure.

Thus, most prospective students anticipated that becoming a student would entail indebtedness, most were concerned about this – women more so than men – and most were probably being unduly optimistic about the amount of money they would owe.

Study 2

Sources of finance

Students were asked which sources of income they were currently receiving. Initial distinctions were made between those students receiving neither a grant nor parental contribution (1%), those with a grant only (23%), those receiving both grant and parental contribution (42%), and those with a parental contribution only (34%)[3].

The highest take-up of student loans (74%) was among the grant only students, though this proportion was not significantly different from the take-up proportions of the 'both' and 'parental contribution only' groups. The grant only group were more likely to be receiving access funds.

Previous experience of borrowing

Students were asked which of the following they had ever borrowed more than £50 from. The proportions of 'yes' responses for different categories were: parents (73%), bank (71%), finance company (39%), friends (33%), other family members (23%), and building society (9%). The number of sources reported by each student (between 0 and 6) was then recoded into three categories, labelled low, medium and high, shown in Table 5.1.

The table shows that 53% of students had taken out a student loan in their first year, 71% of the current second and final year students had one in their second year, and 64% of the final year students had one for

Table 5.1: Effects of previous borrowing on student loan uptake (%)

Number of borrowing sources		Low (0,1)	Medium (2,3)	High (4,5,6)	Total
Student loan in year 1? (All students)	No	40	53	9	47
	Yes	17	52	32	53
Student loan in year 2? (Second and final year students)	No	46	50	5	29
	Yes	14	53	34	71
Student loan in year 3? (Final year students)	No	44	48	8	36
	Yes	9	49	42	64
Total		27	52	21	100

their final year of study. For all three sets of students, those who had greater borrowing experience (that is, had borrowed more than £50 from each of a variety of sources) were significantly more likely to have taken out a student loan. *Chi-square analysis* showed a significant association between the extent of previous borrowing and student loan take-up for each of the three comparisons above.

No data on the amount of income or levels of debt were collected in this study, so it was not possible to examine directly the relative influences of income level and previous experience of indebtedness on the take-up of student loans. For the subsequent analysis reported below, however, the distinction between different funding sources may be taken as a reasonable proxy for parental wealth: grant only students having the poorest parents, grant and parental contribution students having parents with middling disposable income, and parental contribution only students typically having the wealthiest parents.

Worries about student debt

Once at university, the majority of students continued to believe that credit use was an inevitable part of university life. Participants answered a number of questions about their current financial concerns, which were recorded on seven-point scales with labelled endpoints. The proportions of participants answering beyond the mid-point of each scale are given in Table 5.2.

Table 5.2: Participants' current financial concerns

N=223		%
How easy do you think it is for you to avoid taking on a repayable debt while at university?	not easy:	85
How likely do you think it is that you will owe money to a bank or building society at the end of your course?	will owe:	76
To what extent do you feel that any financial difficulties you might have now affect your academic performance?	affecting:	55
How difficult do you think it will be to repay any money you might owe at the end of your course?	difficult:	50
How much control do you feel you have over your financial situation at this point?	not in control:	39
How worried are you about your ability to finance your degree from start to finish?	worried:	37

Table 5.2 shows that 85% of participants claimed that it was not easy to avoid borrowing while at university, and 76% believed they would owe money to a bank or building society by the end of their course. It is also interesting to note that 39% of participants felt they were not in control of their finances, and 37% were worried about their ability to finance their degree from start to finish. Concerning the current and future consequences of credit use, 55% felt that financial difficulties were affecting their academic performance, and 50% thought it would be difficult to repay any money owed at the end of their course. Students anticipated these 'money troubles' as arising from two factors (or sources): poor money management and unforeseen exigencies beyond their apparent control.

Two routes into 'debt'

Factor analysis was used on a section of the questionnaire to reduce 17 possible causes of money troubles to a smaller number of 'dimensions'; two factors were identified[4]. Students who scored highly on Factor 1 rated themselves as more likely to experience money troubles as a result of poor money management techniques including careless budgeting, a lack of self-discipline, wanting to have a good time, an enjoyment of shopping, and the convenience of credit cards. These items can be characterised as typically enduring and internal, that is, they have the properties of psychological traits.

Students who scored highly on Factor 2 by comparison rated themselves as more likely to experience money troubles as a result of a variety of factors that place them under some externally imposed exigencies, which they saw as causing disruption to their student career (for example, illness, bad luck). These items are typically temporary and externally imposed, that is, they can be thought of as psychological states.

1 What best predicts take-up of a student loan?[5]

Although Study 2 did not inquire about actual levels of income, it did ask about sources of income and found that the best single predictor of student loan take-up was not source of income, but extent of previous borrowing experience (whether students were already socialised into a 'borrowing culture'). Of those students who had previously borrowed more than £50 from four or more of parents, bank, finance company, friends, other family members, or building society, 96% had taken out a student loan compared to 63% of the whole sample and 43% of those with little or no previous borrowing. The lowest take-up was among female students with little or no previous experience of borrowing (27%), which contrasted sharply with male students with little or no previous experience of borrowing (62%).

2 Who was most worried about their financial situation?

Taken as a whole, 37% of participants were worried about their financial situation (see Table 5.2), but it was found that the type of financing was the single best predictor of worry. Grant only students were the most susceptible to worry (61%), mixed grant and parental contribution were next (40%), and parental contribution only students were the least worried (23%).

The last group divided down no further, but male and female grant only students differed in how many were worried (50% and 69% respectively). Mixed finance students also divided further: fewer of those without a student loan were worried (23%) than those with a student loan (50%) and among the latter, men (41%) were less susceptible to worry than women (63%).

Thus, female students are generally more worried than male students about financing their degree programmes, except among those students who are likely to be 'better off' – those receiving parental contribution or both parental contribution and a grant, who have not yet needed to take out a student loan – when the sex difference disappears.

3 Who felt 'in control' of their financial situation?

Overall, 39% of students felt that they were 'not in control' of their financial situation (see Table 5.2), and 44% felt 'in control'[6]. The most significant differentiation from this analysis was between those who were and those who were not receiving a student loan; 48% of students with a student loan felt 'not in control' compared to only half that proportion (24%) of those without a loan.

Among participants without a student loan there was further differentiation between those who perceived themselves as possessing good money management skills (73% felt 'in control') and those who saw themselves as having average or poor money management skills (41% 'in control').

Consequently, for those students without a student loan, the extent to which they felt in control of their financial situation was strongly influenced by their perceived money management skills. But for those who had taken out a student loan, the extent to which they felt in control of their present financial situation was quite independent of whether they saw themselves as good, average or poor at managing their finances, their rating of their resourcefulness in this domain being rendered useless.

Having a student loan did not make participants feel in control of their financial situation, in fact the data suggest it might have had the opposite effect (the possibility of causality working in the opposite direction cannot be ruled out – the students who feel 'not in control' may be the ones taking out a student loan). While some students in this group may have felt more in control than they did before, the taking out of a loan did not increase their sense of control to the level of students who had not taken out a loan (54% feeling 'in control').

4 How difficult will it be to repay borrowings on graduation?

When participants were asked how difficult they thought it would be to repay any money they might owe at the end of their degree, 50% thought it would prove difficult (see Table 5.2). Again, the most significant differentiation was between those with a student loan (60% anticipated difficulty) and those without a student loan (34% anticipated difficulty).

Among those with a student loan, more female students (71%) than male students (51%) thought repayment would prove difficult. This pattern was also evident among those without a student loan, with fewer men (19%) than women (42%) thinking repayment would be difficult. Further divisions were also possible with the female students, among whom those who rated themselves as good money managers (69%) were more likely to think repayment would prove difficult than those who rated themselves as average or poor money managers (27%).

Once again, female students proved less confident about their finances and, among those with no loan, those with good self-reported money management skills were being more realistic – and less falsely optimistic – about the repayment of their various borrowings beyond graduation.

Study 3

Sources of finance

Students were asked which sources of income they were currently receiving and an initial distinction was again made between those receiving neither a grant nor a parental contribution (2%), those with grant only (20%), those receiving both grant and parental contribution (36%), and those with parental contribution only (43%)[7]. For this sample, grant only students received the least, and parental contribution only students the most, non-repayable 'gift' income; and all three groups took on comparable levels of borrowings, preserving the differences in available disposable moneys[8].

Overall, 40% of these students had a student loan, 42% a bank or building society overdraft, and 29% were utilising savings as a current source of finance. The highest take-up of student loans was among grant only students, 72% of whom had taken one out.

Anticipated student debt and its psychological effects

Students were asked not only their currently anticipated student debt on graduation (graduate debt), but also to indicate what level they considered 'manageable' and what they considered to be 'excessive'. This allowed the division of participants into three types according to where they placed their anticipated graduate debt with respect to their 'manageable' and 'excessive' levels of debt.

A new variable termed 'Graduate Debt Type' (GDT) was created with scores 1, 2 or 3 where 1 represented students who saw their anticipated graduate debt as 'manageable' (19%), 2 represented students who saw their anticipated graduate debt as 'intermediate' (62%), and 3 represented students who saw their anticipated graduate debt as 'excessive' (19%).

One-way analysis of variance showed significant differences between GDTs for all three estimates, which have been plotted in Figure 5.1[9]. Figure 5.1 shows that Type 1 students saw their anticipated graduate debt as manageable because the amount they anticipated owing (middle column) was relatively low, and the amount they considered manageable (left column) was relatively high. Conversely, Type 3 students saw their anticipated graduate debt as excessive because the amount they anticipated owing was relatively high while what they deemed to be

Figure 5.1: Mean levels of manageable, anticipated and excessive graduate debt of Graduate Debt Type 1, 2 and 3 students

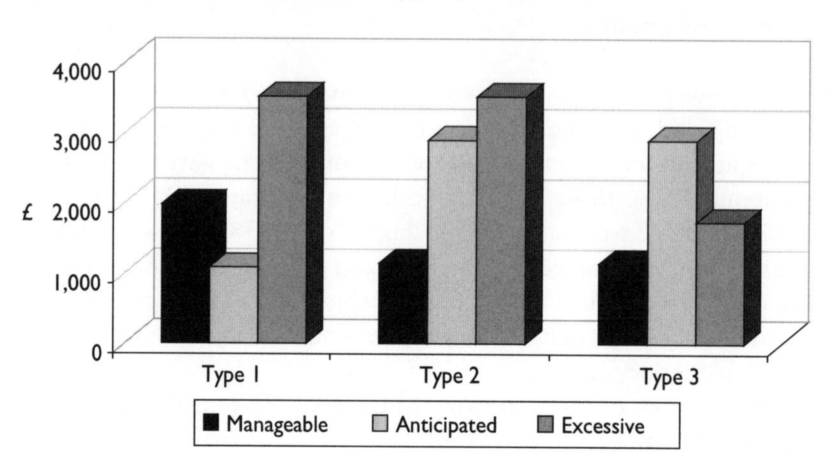

excessive was relatively low (right column). Type 2, then, represented an intermediate position because although the amount they anticipated owing was relatively high, indeed higher than the amount they considered manageable, the amount they believed to be excessive was even higher. For Types 2 and 3 therefore, their graduate debt was not manageable, whereas for Types 1 and 2 it was not excessive. Types 1 and 2 did not differ statistically in the average value of the upper limit, but they did differ in how much they anticipated owing and in whether that exceeded their lower limit or not. Types 2 and 3 by comparison did not differ statistically in how much they anticipated owing, but they did differ psychologically in whether this level of debt seemed excessive or not.

This 'psychological' variable, focusing on students' interpretations of their likely graduate debt, proved to be a powerful predictor of their financial concerns across a wide variety of questionnaire items including levels of anxiety, levels of depression, who was most worried about their financial situation, who felt 'in control' of their financial situation, how difficult it would be to repay the money owed on graduation, and who saw themselves as currently in financial difficulties. It is to these topics of discussion that we now turn[10].

Predicting levels of anxiety

Anxiety and depression were measured using the hospital anxiety and depression (HAD) scale items developed by Zigmond and Snaith (1983).

The authors suggest cut-off points for distinguishing between those with normal (low), borderline (intermediate), and pathological (high) levels of distress. Overall, of those students who had scores on all relevant variables (n=115), 30% showed normal levels of anxiety, 17% were at borderline level, and 53% at pathological level. The best single predictor of membership of these three groups was again GDT and 74% of Type 3 (who anticipated their student debt on graduation to be 'excessive') reported pathological levels of anxiety. Of those who saw their graduate debt as not excessive (Types 1 and 2), 45% reported high-level anxiety, and this was significantly further differentiated between Arts students (62% reported pathological anxiety), and Science and Engineering, and Economic and Social Science students (31% reported pathological anxiety).

Thus, half the students in this sample reported high levels of anxiety. This was statistically independent of sex and year of study, and was not systematically affected by the amount of income available that year, or by the amount they anticipated owing either for that year or on graduation. However, for those who saw their anticipated student debt on graduation to be (in their own terms and by their own metric) 'excessive', over half as many again reported high anxiety. Among those who saw their anticipated graduate debt as 'not excessive' (whether 'manageable' or in the 'grey area' between manageable and excessive), Arts students were twice as likely to be showing anxiety.

Predicting levels of depression

Overall, 15% of the students were pathologically depressed (the considerably higher incidence of anxiety compared with depression is in line with population incidence figures). Again, the single best predictor of depression group membership was GDT, with 32% of Type 3 (who anticipated their student debt on graduation to be excessive) reporting pathological levels of depression. Of those who saw their graduate debt as not excessive (Types 1 and 2) only 8% reported high levels of depression, and this was significantly further differentiated between non-science students (14% reported pathological depression) and Science and Engineering students (none of whom reported depression at this level).

Anticipating that student debt on graduation would be excessive, doubled the numbers reporting high levels of depression. Again, beyond the second level distinction where faculty interacted with GDT, neither demographic nor economic variables made any further differentiation.

Attitudes to finances and life at university

Students responded to a number of attitude statements on five-point agree–disagree scales with labelled endpoints. The percentages of those agreeing with, indifferent to, and disagreeing with each of these statements is given in Table 5.3.

1 Who was most worried about their financial situation?

In Study 2 the best predictor of financial worry proved to be the type of financing the student was receiving: grant only, mixed, or parental only. In this study, type of financing again proved to be important, but now only after the more statistically significant effects of the new variable GDT had been entered.

Table 5.3: Proportions of agreement and disagreement with attitude statements (%)

N=199	Agree		Disagree
In the long term I will benefit financially from a university education	74	19	7
In general I feel in control of my financial situation*	64	21	15
I expect my financial situation to improve in the next five years	63	14	23
Realistically, I would have enough to live on if I were just a bit more careful in how I spent my money	44	7	49
I am worried about my ability to repay my debts after graduation*	42	9	49
I feel I have only myself to blame for any financial difficulties I get into as a student	29	15	56
I am worried about how I am going to finance the rest of my undergraduate degree course*	29	15	56
I expect my financial situation to improve in the next 12 months	26	22	52
I am currently in financial difficulties*	20	19	61
The state of my finances has had an adverse effect on my academic performance this year	16	18	66
I have thought seriously about dropping out of university because of financial hardship	7	6	87

Notes: Scale 'agree' 1 + 2, 'disagree' 4 + 5; *further reference will be made to the statements in **bold**.

Thirty-four per cent of students were worried about their financial situation. Of the GDT 1 students (who perceived their anticipated student debt on graduation as 'manageable') 11% were, nonetheless, worried. Among Types 2 and 3 (not 'manageable') students, of those receiving a grant only, 72% were worried, whereas of those receiving a parental contribution (whether both grant and parental contribution, or parental contribution only) 31% were worried.

2 Who felt 'in control' of their financial situation?

In this sample 56% agreed that they generally felt in control of their financial situation. Among GDT 3 students, however, only 29% felt 'in control'. At the opposite extreme, 87% of first year students, not anticipating much end-of-year student debt, and not anticipating an 'excessive' level of graduate debt, felt 'in control'.

3 How difficult will it be to repay borrowings on graduation?

Of participants, 53% were worried about their ability to repay the money they owed after graduation. Only 9% of those reporting their anticipated graduate debt as 'manageable' (GDT 1), however, were worried, providing some measure of corroboration of the GDT measure.

For this dependent variable a number of factors made statistically significant ($p<.05$) level one differentiation (anticipated amount of graduate debt; end-of-year student debt; type of financing – grant only vs parental contribution; presence of student loan; total annual income), but GDT gave the most significant differentiation.

4 Who saw themselves as currently in financial difficulties?

Overall, 26% of this sample owned up to being in financial difficulty and although a number of the factors were significant at the first level of analysis, the best single factor was anticipated end-of-year student debt. Where this was low, only 10% saw themselves as being in difficulty. Where anticipated end-of-year student debt was medium or high in comparison to the rest of the sample, 50% of those financed by grant only felt themselves to be in difficulty, whereas this figure reduced to

22% of those receiving a parental contribution (whether both grant and parental contribution or parental contribution only).

Predicting membership of GDTs 1, 2 and 3

The most significant factor in determining GDT (omitting anticipated graduate debt, which is involved in the computation of GDT) was whether or not the student currently held a student loan. This is shown in Figure 5.2.

Thus, whereas of this sample 57% overall held a student loan, among those anticipating their burden of student debt on graduation to be excessive (GDT 3), 84% held a student loan.

Figure 5.2: Proportions of Graduate Debt Type 1, 2 and 3 students with and without a student loan

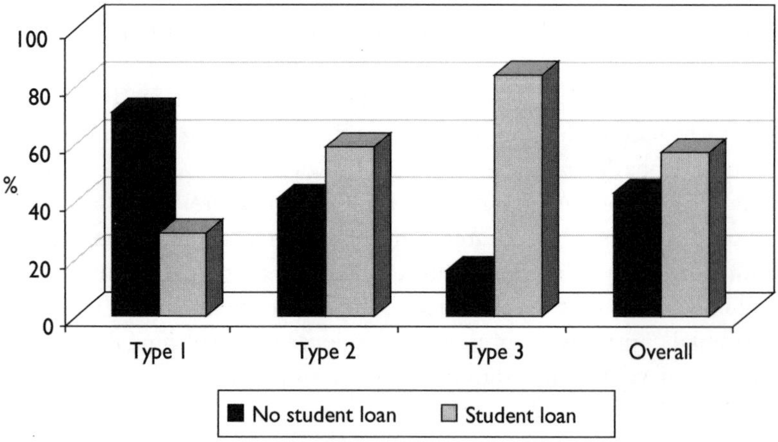

Conclusion

Most prospective students anticipated that becoming a student would entail indebtedness, most were concerned about this (women more so than men) and most were probably being unduly optimistic about the amount they would owe.

Once at university, students continued to be worried about the likelihood of ending their student career in debt with 85% claiming that it was not easy to avoid borrowing and 76% believing they would owe money to a bank or building society by the time they completed their course. About half of the students also felt that financial difficulties were affecting their academic performance and thought it would be difficult to repay any money owed at the end of their course. Money troubles were seen as arising from one of two general sources: poor money management skills such as careless budgeting, lack of self-discipline and enjoyment of shopping; and unforeseen exigencies beyond their apparent control such as being under stress, a high cost of living, and illness.

When considering levels of debt, it was found that students' state of mind concerning their student debt was best predicted not by 'economic' indicators such as the simple amount of annual income or of the amount they anticipated owing, but by their 'psychological' interpretations of their situation, and it was this interpretation that constitutes the psychological 'burden of debt' that increasing numbers of students now carry through their student career and will continue to carry beyond graduation.

The most significant factor in determining the membership of GDTs 1, 2 or 3 was whether the student had a student loan: among those anticipating their level of debt on graduation to be excessive 84% held a student loan, and among those anticipating their level of debt on graduation to be manageable 29% held a student loan.

Taking out a student loan obviously increases disposable income yet the results of this research suggest it does not remove, and may indeed exacerbate, the psychological 'burden of debt' people carry during their student career, and anticipate carrying after graduation.

Notes

[1] More detailed information concerning the research methods is included in Appendix A.

[2] All statistical analysis techniques written in *italics* are included in the glossary (Appendix B).

[3] One per cent represented two students, one of whom was living on a scholarship, the other on sponsorship and vacation work.

[4] The *factor analysis* of the sources of money troubles is provided in Table F1 (Appendix F).

[5] *Chi-square automatic interaction detection (CHAID)*, which identifies independent 'predictors' of group membership, was used to address this question and the three that follow.

[6] The remainder had no opinion.

[7] Two per cent represented three students, one claiming support from a partner at £3,600 per annum, one declaring a student loan and claiming to make £4,500 per annum, and one with no visible means of support!

[8] 'Gift' income incorporated government grants, parental contributions and access funds.

[9] *Scheffé post-hoc tests* were used to locate the significant differences between groups, and where these showed no difference between two types, the actual means have been replaced by the mean for the two groups combined.

[10] Once again *CHAID* was used for the remaining results.

Part III:
An international perspective

SIX

Student attitudes towards credit and debt: a cross-national study between Italy and the UK

Gaia Vicenzi, Stephen E.G. Lea, and Rino Rumiati

Introduction

So far, this book has concentrated on the UK, where the use of credit is increasingly common among the student population. This situation has developed gradually since around 1990, and to some extent it is possible to study its development by looking at the situation at different points over the past 10 years. Studies reported in this book do allow at least some 'tracking' of the student debt phenomenon in this way. Although it is not possible to go back in time and ask questions of students of what might be called the 'pre-debt' period, cross-national studies enable something similar to this.

Although student debt is a widespread phenomenon, it is not worldwide. This chapter compares the experience and understanding of credit use among students from the UK and Italy. Student debt is practically unknown in Italy, and there has never been much in the way of financial support for students. There are no loans from the government, banks do not offer special loan systems to students, and in the majority of cases parents are required to act as guarantor for students who ask for a loan. In addition, it is rare to find a bank that allows students to have an overdraft. Consequently, Italian students are very dependent on their families, who represent their principal source of income, and this situation has not changed in recent years.

This chapter is not a neutral comparison of borrowing experiences and attitudes of students in the two countries. Rather, it is an attempt at time travelling. The questions about student debt that are posed by the experiences of UK students have been asked in the Italian context. That is to say, methodologically, the empirical work was driven by what is already known about UK students; no previous psychological research specifically relating to student debt has been conducted in Italy.

Of course, in any cross-national comparison, multiple differences come into play. Being a student in Italy today is far from identical to being a student in the UK in 1990. For example, it is important to note that the likelihood of graduate employment in Italy is much lower than in the UK: in 1995 the unemployment rate in Italy for graduates aged between 25 and 34 was 21% compared to 4% in the UK (Education Training Youth, 1997).

The present chapter takes as its starting point the work of Davies and Lea on students' attitudes towards credit and debt in relation to their experiences. Davies and Lea (1995) showed that both levels of debt and tolerant attitudes towards credit and debt increase over the three years of the typical UK undergraduate's degree programme. Some other research on borrowing (for example, Tokunaga, 1993) has suggested that locus of control, particularly if measured using an economic locus of control scale (for example, Furnham, 1986) may be correlated with either attitude or behaviour towards credit and debt. Furthermore, the dominant life-cycle models of financial behaviour suggest that both saving and debt would depend to some extent on events within an individual's life. Accordingly, in the present investigation, scales of economic locus of control and life events were used in order to see whether they would improve the prediction of either attitudes or behaviour towards credit and debt, and to control for the possibility that any apparent national differences in attitudes towards credit and debt could derive from differences in these more fundamental variables.

For the same reasons, some questions about spending patterns, which Morgan, Roberts and Powdrill (Chapter Two), and Lea, Webley and Bellamy (Chapter Three) have shown to be related to levels of debt, were also included. In light of Davies and Lea's research, levels of debt and attitudes towards credit and debt were examined within three student samples: two from Italy and one from the UK. Two Italian samples were used so that students from public universities could be compared with students from private universities. This comparison is important because students attending private universities generally have higher incomes than those attending public universities, and it has been noted that levels of debt and attitudes towards credit and debt are frequently correlated with economic prosperity (Katona, 1964).

The samples and the questionnaires[1]

The UK sample consisted of 38 first year, 40 second year and 43 third year undergraduate students from the University of Exeter. The Italian sample consisted of 97 first year, 99 second year, 80 third year and 88 fourth year undergraduate students from the Universities of Milano, Padova and Pavia. In addition, 89 student 'drop outs' were also included as they are very common in Italy compared to the UK, where their proportion is typically less than 5%. The total sample was approximately matched for gender, and mature students were excluded (those over 25 in the UK and over 28 in Italy).

The questionnaire was very similar to the one used by Davies and Lea (1995). It contained basic demographic items, three psychological scales, and questions about the participant's financial position and financial habits. The attitude scale of Davies and Lea had to be modified as two of the original statements were not suitable for the Italian sample and four further statements were removed to improve the reliability score. The remaining eight statements used for statistical analysis are included in Table 6.1.

The questionnaire also included a student life events scale (Sarason et al, 1978) and an economic locus of control scale (Furnham, 1986). Other questions considered basic socio-demographic items, economic socialisation, money management and perceptions of financial positions, levels and sources of income, estimated expenditures, and levels of debt.

Table 6.1: Statements retained from the Davies and Lea (1995) attitude scale for use in analysis

	Statement
1.	There is no excuse for borrowing money
2.	It is okay to borrow money in order to buy food
3.	You should always save up first before buying something
4.	It is okay to have an overdraft if you know you can pay it off
5.	Once you are in debt it is very difficult to get out
6.	You should stay home rather than borrow money to go out for an evening in the pub
7.	It is better to have something now and pay for it later
8.	Owing money is basically wrong

Results and discussion[2]

Some extreme values concerning total income, expenditure and levels of debt were dropped from the analysis to avoid distorting or masking more general trends. Examples include two students from the UK, one reporting an income of £18,000 and debts amounting to £12,000, the other reporting a total expenditure of £15,300. Five extreme values concerning levels of debt were also dropped from the Italian sample, shifting the 'mean total borrowings' from 3.522 to 2.014 million lire (four of the five values dropped were from students attending private universities).

Basis for country comparisons

When comparing monetary values between the two countries the price of McDonald's' 'Big Macs' was used (ITL 8,900 = £1.90, that is, ITL 4,684 = £1). Comparison of the prices of key student consumer goods showed that comparing values by the financial exchange rate (ITL 2,854 = £1) would have grossly overstated the purchasing power of UK students. It has been forcefully argued by economists that the 'Big Mac Index' provides a better comparison of consumer purchasing power than the financial exchange rate (for example, Click, 1996; Ong, 1997).

Even with this less favourable exchange rate, *t-test analysis* showed that the UK sample spent more on non-essential items (especially on alcohol and cigarettes) ($p<.01$), and received higher incomes ($p<.01$) than the Italian sample.

Proportions of students in debt: the two countries separately

As can be seen from Table 6.2, there was only a modest difference between the mean levels of total borrowing in the UK and Italy (£264); this difference was not statistically significant.

The average figure, however, conceals within it major national differences: 55% of the UK sample reported some debt compared with 13% of the Italian sample (10% in the public university subsample and 16% in the private university subsample). Because of the comparatively small number of Italian students in debt, the two subsamples were combined for the first stage of the statistical analysis and for comparisons between the UK and Italy; this is appropriate because the distinction

Table 6.2: Average income, expenditure and student debt in the UK and Italy (£)

	UK			ITALY				
	Without debt	In debt	Total	Public university	Private university	Without debt	In debt	Total
Total income	4,222	4,377	4,276	1,222	2,165	1,500	2,406	1,649
Essential expenditure	1,153	1,477	1,339	832	1,348	1,041	1,336	1,084
Non-essential expenditure	1,445	1,821	1,655	783	1,010	855	1,144	895
Total expenditure	2,598	3,298	2,994	1,615	2,358	1,896	2,480	1,979
% in debt	–	–	55%	10%	16%	–	–	13%
Total student debt	–	–	843	571	579	–	–	579

between public and private universities does not exist in the UK. Differences between the two Italian subsamples formed a second stage of analysis.

First, how did the results in both the UK and Italy compare with those obtained by Davies and Lea (1995) who conducted their research in the same UK university but seven years earlier? In contrast with their results, the proportion of students in debt in the UK sample did not increase greatly across year groups (31% first year, 37% second, and 37% third). In the Italian sample, the number of students in debt did not increase across year groups either, but more surprising perhaps was the inconsistent distributions of students in debt (16% first year, 24% second, 16% third, 16% fourth, and 27% of 'drop out' students).

Second, was being in debt the same sort of phenomenon for students in the two countries? This question was addressed by looking at the factors that tended to be correlated with being in debt in the two countries. *Stepwise logistic regression* was used to explore which of the variables significantly distinguished students in debt from students without debt. Separate analyses were carried out for the UK and Italian samples and then on the combined sample.

- In the UK sample, 85.6% of cases were correctly classified and students in debt were discriminated by being male (p<.05), having less income

($p<.05$), having a more tolerant attitude towards credit and debt ($p<.01$), and having more strategies to alleviate their financial position ($p<.05$). No significant differences were found for student loan take-up or having a credit card.

- In the Italian sample, 87.9% of the cases were correctly classified and students in debt were discriminated by having a credit card ($p<.01$) and having more strategies to alleviate their financial position ($p<.05$). When the credit card variable was excluded from the analysis (since it could have been determined by some of the other variables), students in debt were found to use more strategies to alleviate their financial position ($p<.01$), to be more likely to have an external locus of control ($p<.05$), and to feel more confident about securing employment after graduation ($p<.05$).
- Looking at the public university students only among the Italian sample, it was found that those in debt had higher incomes than those without debt ($p<.05$). It is important to note, however, that there was a high proportion of missing values for 'income' among the Italian students, whether this was taken as 'estimated annual incomes' (29% missing) or 'estimated income from different sources' (44% missing). This situation could be a reflection of the principal source of students' financial support – their family. In Italy, students rarely receive a monthly allowance and often do not know how much they cost their parents: 77% of students received money from their parents, 35% being unable to say how much.

Proportions of students in debt: the two countries compared

The combined sample was used to identify a set of variables on which the two national samples should be compared. *Stepwise logistic regression* was able to classify 81.3% of cases correctly, and students in debt were discriminated by having a credit card ($p<.01$), using more strategies to alleviate their financial position ($p<.01$), having a more favourable attitude towards credit and debt ($p<.05$), and having greater 'essential' expenditures ($p<.05$). Comparisons on these variables between the two national samples by *t-test analysis* showed that, overall, students from the UK and Italy differed considerably on all four. These differences, however, were no longer significant when only those students in debt were considered. This strongly suggests that these variables are related to credit use regardless of the great institutional differences between the two countries, and that the apparent national difference is simply due to the reality that far more UK than Italian students are in debt. It is also interesting to note that among those Italian students who were in debt and attending private university, credit card ownership was more usual ($p<.01$) and essential expenditure was greater ($p<.01$).

The only factor that was associated with being in debt both in the UK and in Italy was 'using more strategies to alleviate their financial position', and this therefore deserves further discussion. Student examples include, "I gave myself a fixed spending budget" and "I monitor my bank statements and expenditure closely". This finding is particularly interesting when related to Davies and Lea's finding that students in debt worried less about their bank account than those who were without debt; it suggests that students in debt have changed their financial behaviour over the seven-year period between the two studies, perhaps because a different kind of student now has to incur debt. On the basis of the findings it might be argued that now, students who are in debt are worried about their position, are conscious of this concern, and try to reduce their debt through the use of various strategies as a result. Whether these strategies actually work is a separate issue. When looking at the UK sample one would be inclined to agree with the findings of Bellamy (1994) who argued that the financial strategies adopted by students were unsuccessful because levels of debt continued to increase across year groups. In this light, the behaviour of the Italian students, even those who did have some debt, looks different. They showed no such increase in levels of debt across year groups. It would be interesting to see if Italian students are more successful in their financial management than their UK counterparts, but to investigate this demands a more qualitative approach than was possible in the present study.

In line with previous research it was found that, overall, students in debt were more likely to be male. Although this association between gender and being in debt was not statistically significant in Italy (probably because of the small numbers who had any debt at all), the finding that men in both countries had the highest levels of debt is discussed later.

An interesting disparity between the two countries was that students in debt from the UK tended to have low incomes, while students in debt from Italy tended to have high incomes. It is emphasised by the reality that Italian students with the highest levels of debt came from private universities (where income levels are higher), and those students from public universities who were in debt tended to have higher incomes than their peers. It will be argued below that this disparity contains the key to understanding the observed national differences. But first, the data on levels of debt (among those who had any debt at all) need to be considered.

Levels of indebtedness among those in debt

Among those who had any borrowings at all, the patterns of debt across years were different between the two countries. In the UK sample, mean levels of debt increased across year groups (£575 first year, £703 second year, and £1,151 third year), whereas in the Italian sample, levels of debt varied dramatically between year groups but with no discernible pattern (2.201 million lire in the first year, 1.530 million in the second year, 1.250 million in the third year, 3.477 million in the fourth year, and 1.903 million for 'drop out' students). Also, students from public and private Italian universities showed no significant differences in the levels of debt.

As with the issue of being in debt, the same variables were looked at to see whether they were associated with having more or less debt in the two countries; students who had no debt were dropped from these analyses. *Stepwise linear regression* was therefore used to explore these questions, again carrying out analyses separately for UK and Italian samples.

- Among the UK students in debt, as shown in Figure 6.1, it was found that being in the final year of study, being male, and not feeling confident about securing employment after graduation were all associated with higher levels of debt ($p<.05$).

Figure 6.1: Path analysis of factors associated with levels of debt among UK students

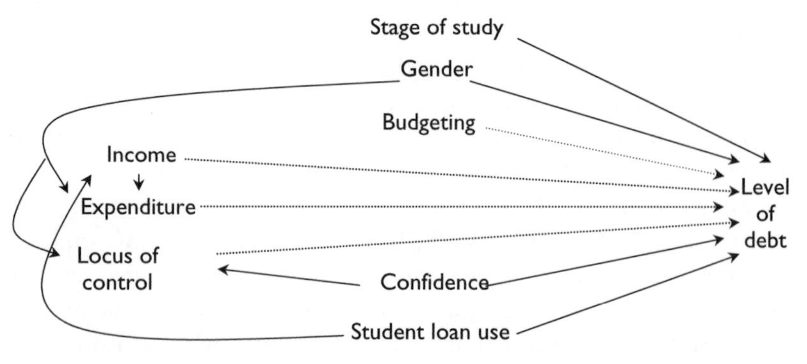

Note: ⟶ Significant associations; ⋯⋯→ Non-significant associations.

Figure 6.2: Path analysis of factors associated with levels of debt among Italian students

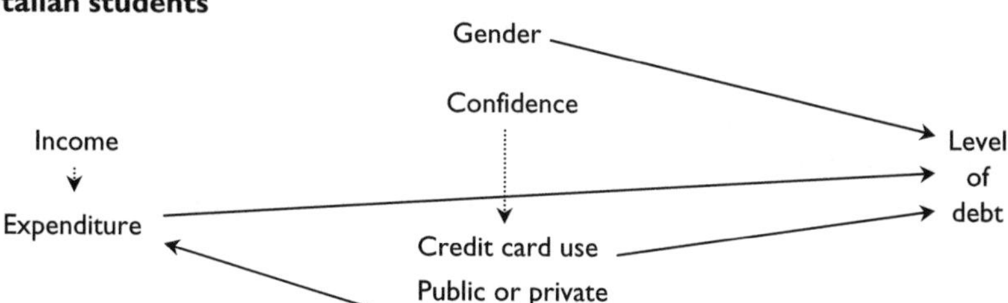

- Figure 6.2 shows that among the Italian students in debt, it was found that being male, having a credit card, having greater expenditures (both essential and non-essential), feeling confident about securing employment after graduation, and attending a private university were all associated with higher levels of debt (among those having any borrowings at all).

These results support those from the analysis of whether or not students were in debt: given that they were in debt, having higher levels of debt were found among those with higher income in Italy but among those with lower income in the UK.

Why are there national differences in debt behaviour?

The detailed statistical analysis has suggested that debt is quite a different phenomenon among Italian than among UK students. The UK findings, both for whether students have any debt and for the amount they have, if they have any at all, fit in with previous research that suggests credit use is influenced by having a low income (Lea, Webley and Bellamy, Chapter Three; Webley et al, 1993). But the Italian findings run in the opposite direction, and this is harder to understand. A possible explanation comes from work of Katona (1975) that showed, within the population at large, individuals with higher incomes were the most likely to borrow money in a given year, and if they did borrow, did so by the largest amounts. On this analogy, student debt in Italy should be looked at as being 'credit use' and thought of as a luxury that only the wealthiest students can afford. Italian students in debt would then correspond to the small subgroup of student 'credit users' identified by

Lea, Webley and Bellamy (Chapter Three), and indeed they constitute a comparable proportion of the sample. As already shown, they were also concentrated in the private universities. It would be expected that the wealthier students would be in these institutions, and some statistical findings support this assumption. Analyses using *t-test analysis* showed that students from public university felt less optimistic about their employment after graduation ($p<.01$), and found credit card ownership more unusual ($p<.01$) than students from private university. It was also found that students from public university received less income than students from private university ($p<.01$).

To interpret this difference further, it will be helpful to consider the different distributions of social status among the two samples. Although this was not found to be a significant variable in predicting credit use, its impact is likely to have differed between the samples, as the UK students were a more socially homogeneous group than their Italian counterparts. The greater part of the UK student sample (76%) came from the highest social level (professional and managerial), and it can reasonably be argued that because of their apparent similarity, the UK sample was affected by a 'social comparison' phenomenon (Festinger, 1954): the less wealthy members of the group felt the need to spend the same levels of money as the wealthier ones, since they identified with them. In a study of US bankruptcy records, Sullivan et al (1989) have shown that it is low income relative to someone's perceived social group, rather than absolute low income, that seems to predict whether they will suffer bankruptcy. Furthermore, since the use of credit is widely perceived to be the 'norm' among UK students (reasonably enough, because a lot of students do indeed borrow money), social comparisons might lead directly to students taking out loans, as well as leading to borrowing indirectly by way of expenditure patterns. In this sense, student borrowing might itself be described as a consumer good that the poorer student cannot actually afford, whereas the wealthiest students, Lea, Webley and Bellamy's 'credit users' perhaps (Chapter Three), actually can.

In Italy, by comparison, especially in public universities, students were more representative of the spread of social status in the population as a whole (Social Class 1 constituted 21% of the sample; Class 2, 3%; Class 3, 4%; Class 4, 11%; Class 5, 23%; and Class 6, 38%)[3]. Consequently, social comparison would be less likely to lead students into debt as the student group was not homogeneous enough to bring about an 'inter-individual intra-group' comparison. Furthermore, students in debt represented a small minority that could not be considered the norm.

As shown among the Italian but not the UK students, there was a correlation between the highest levels of debt and the highest levels of spending. Furthermore, Italian students in debt and students with high levels of debt were confident about securing employment after their degree, and students from private university were more optimistic about their future careers than students from public university. In the UK by comparison, students in debt and students with high levels of debt were characterised by a lack of confidence surrounding their future employment. One might argue that the wealthier Italian students used credit because they were used to a comfortable lifestyle and were reluctant to give it up, regardless of the lifestyles of their colleagues. Willingness to borrow might also be influenced by the confidence of Italian students in relation to their chances of future employment: it is plausible that the wealthiest students, who would be the children of wealthy families, would stand the best chance of obtaining well-paid jobs, because of their 'social capital' (see Webley et al, 2001).

Explanations of student debt in the two countries

Thus in the Italian situation, it is reasonable to turn to the life-cycle hypothesis (LCH) (Ando and Modigliani, 1963) for an explanation of student debt: students behave as if they see university as an investment in terms of their future employment and are willing to borrow more readily as a result.

The UK situation, however, is a little more difficult to interpret. On the one hand, it might be that students in debt are from less 'well-off' families and subsequently have less guaranteed employment opportunities after graduation ('well-off' parents are more likely to have either their own company or business contacts). On the other hand, it might be that students start borrowing because, as in Italy, they feel confident about being able to repay the money after graduation, but as levels of debt increase their confidence subsides, they become anxious and adopt a pessimistic outlook on their future. An association, found in the UK only, was that students in their final year of study tended to have higher levels of debt. This finding supports the research of Davies and Lea (1995) and most likely reflects the cumulative effect of necessary borrowing in the UK, which would not arise in Italy under the hypothesis that credit use among Italian students is a luxury that only the relatively wealthy incur.

An association, found in Italy but not in the UK, was that students in debt and students with high levels of debt tended to have a credit card. Previous research has also shown this apparent relationship between borrowing and credit card use in both the UK and the US (for example, Davies and Lea, 1995; Feinberg, 1986). A possible explanation for the current lack of association in the UK sample is a simple ceiling effect – a high proportion of students now own one or more credit cards. As a consequence, having a credit card is no longer a discriminating factor for high levels of debt as in Italy where only 22% of students had a credit card.

Attitudes towards credit and debt

It seems, therefore, that the phenomenon of student debt differs markedly between the UK and Italy. The results also show that attitudes differ between the two countries: students from the UK had significantly more favourable attitudes towards credit and debt than students from Italy ($p<.05$). The patterns of correlations with attitudes also differed.

In the UK, attitudes towards credit and debt became more favourable across year groups (attitude scores shifting from 'no opinion' in the first year to a more favourable credit and debt attitude in the third and fourth years). *Regression analysis* was used to try to pin down what variables were correlated with variations in attitudes and showed that being in the final year of study, being male, and not using strategies to alleviate their financial position were all significantly associated with more favourable attitudes ($p<.05$), as shown in Figure 6.3. High total expenditure was also found to correlate with favourable attitudes towards credit and debt. Although there were no significant differences between 'essential' and 'non-essential' expenditure patterns, this could be the result of items like 'food' and 'clothing' changing categories as income changes: for a relatively prosperous student, such items could become hedonistic (bought for pleasure) rather than utilitarian (bought out of necessity). It is well documented that as people become better off they tend to shift from eating at home to 'eating out' (for example, Scitovsky, 1976).

In the Italian sample, attitudes towards credit and debt were on the favourable side of the scale, with fourth year students, the students with the highest levels of debt, having the most tolerant attitudes[4]. Perhaps surprisingly, no difference was observed between students from private and public universities. Among the subsample who did have some debt, attending a private university, having an external locus of control,

Figure 6.3: Path analysis of factors associated with tolerant attitudes towards credit and debt among UK students

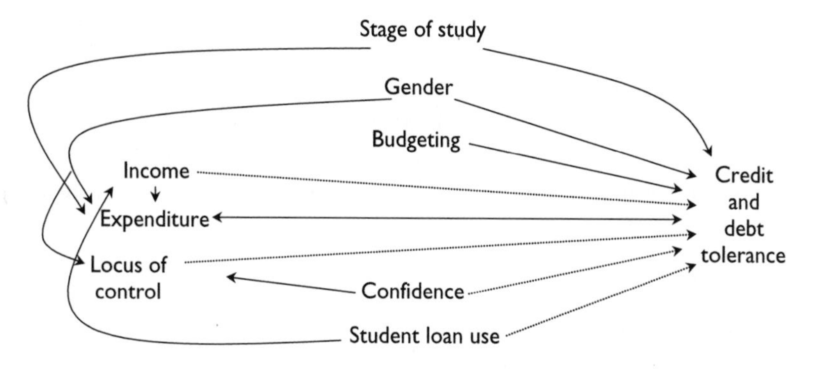

Note: ⟶ Significant associations; ┈┈➝ Non-significant associations.

Figure 6.4: Path analysis of factors associated with tolerant attitudes towards credit and debt among Italian students

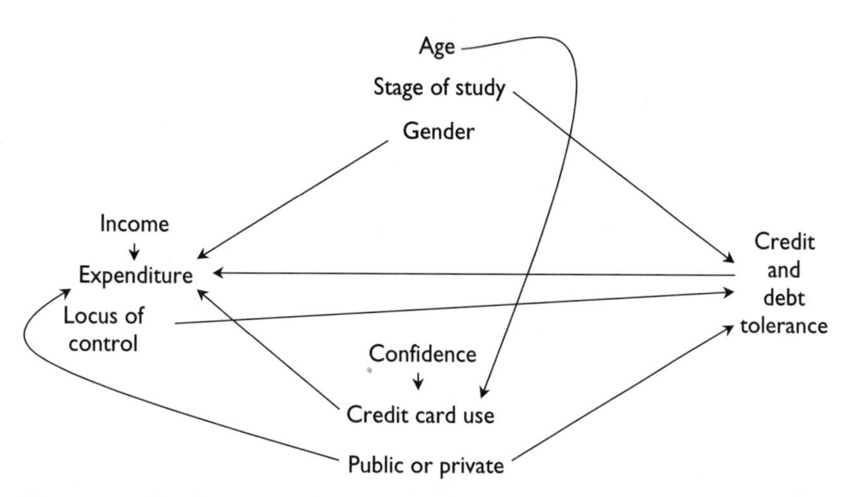

Note: ⟶ Significant associations; ┈┈➝ Non-significant associations.

and being in the last year of study were all associated with more favourable attitudes ($p<.05$), included in Figure 6.4. The first of these correlations supports the previous assertion that in Italy student debt is linked more closely to 'wealth' than 'poverty'.

Note that in both the UK and Italy, students in their final year of study tended to have more favourable attitudes towards credit and debt, a finding that again supports the results of Davies and Lea (1995). Also in line with previous research was the finding that those UK students who were in debt had more favourable attitudes towards credit and debt. More interestingly, however, was the finding that this relationship did not exist in Italy. This finding leads to questions relating to the origins of attitudes towards credit and debt in the two countries.

The average UK first year student responded as having 'no opinion' regarding credit and debt. This may be regarded as a naive response, probably reflecting these students' lack of borrowing experience prior to entering university. Similarly, in the entire Italian sample, it was found that very few variables were actually associated with attitudes towards credit and debt (looking at the subsample of students in debt, the only significant correlation was with locus of control). Furthermore, statistically the attitude scales had low reliability (that is, answers to the different questions often disagreed), and this suggests that there was only weak evidence that the different questions in the scale were accessing any coherent mental concept in the minds of the people filling in the questionnaire. In Italy, it might be argued that the act of being in debt is so unusual that attitudes towards credit and debt relate to a theoretical notion rather than a tangible problem.

Although some changes have been identified across the seven-year interval between the two studies, the main trends found for the UK students in the present study agree with the results of Davies and Lea (1995): both levels of debt and favourable attitudes towards credit and debt increased during students' three years at university. It would appear that some form of borrowing is increasingly inevitable in the UK right from the beginning of university, as there was no significant increase in the number of students in debt across year groups. It is likely that most first year students would have heard about debt, some encouragingly and others discouragingly, but most would not have experienced borrowing directly. Then, having entered university, they incurred some debt, the levels of which got higher and higher, until they came to accept that they could not stop its growth. It is at this point that they alter their attitudes to become more favourable towards credit and debt to be in line with their borrowing behaviour. Such an explanation is consistent with the 'cognitive dissonance theory' (Festinger, 1957) of attitudes towards credit and debt favoured by Davies and Lea, where students are forced to change their attitudes because they are unable to alter their behaviour (that is, avoid credit use).

But why, therefore, should Italian students have overall favourable attitudes towards credit and debt, since they have little or no experience of it? It may be that they simply have too little experience of credit use at any stage to formulate any accurate attitudes towards it; or that because borrowing is associated with a wealthy lifestyle, it acquires a favourable image that would be quickly tarnished for the majority of students, assuming they came into contact with it. But these explanations can only be speculative at this stage.

Country comparisons and time travelling

Has it been possible, as hoped, to use the UK–Italy comparison to travel back in time, as it were, and look at what the UK situation might have been like if the policy changes of the 1990s had not taken place? Or do the results reflect pervasive differences between the UK and Italy that have little to do with the different modes of student finance now operating in the two countries?

Some aspects of the results do undoubtedly reflect enduring cultural differences. The lower apparent role of social comparisons among Italian students seems to reflect a less well defined class-based student identity in Italy than in the UK, and this is something that would have been, if anything, stronger in the UK of the 1980s than now, since UK higher education has become more of a mass phenomenon in recent years.

For the most part, however, the differences between UK and Italian students do seem to be plausible reflections of the effects of 10 years of an enforced culture of student debt in the UK. In a variety of ways, credit use for Italian students is a reflection of an unusual, wealthy lifestyle; it is something the rich can afford and the rest do not aspire to, though they may in a way admire it. For UK students, it has become an unpleasant reality, mistrusted by those who have not yet experienced it themselves, increasingly tolerated by those who have had to use it, but certainly not considered exotic or admirable.

Notes

[1] More detailed information concerning the research methods is included in Appendix A.

[2] All statistical analysis techniques written in *italics* are included in the glossary (Appendix B).

[3] It should be noted that Class 1 represents the lowest class according to the international standard classification of occupations (International Labour Office, 1968).

[4] These results should be interpreted with caution because of the low reliability score obtained.

SEVEN

Are students serious bankers? The nature of the student–bank relationship in the UK and France

Will Lebens and Alan Lewis

Introduction

This chapter combines a UK study with a second cross-national investigation, this time between the UK and France. In contrast to previous studies, rather than focusing on credit and debt directly, this chapter is concerned with student attitudes towards banks. It sets out to identify key themes in the student–bank relationship and the implications of increasing student debt on this relationship.

Finance has always been an issue of central importance for students in the UK. Equally important, as their main point of financial contact, are their banks. Since 1990, changes in the structure of the student economy have emerged which have had direct implications for the student–bank relationship. Banks used to relish the custom of students for their guaranteed income at the start of every term, and students found 'allies' in banks because their relationship was relatively simple and (potentially) of little consequence. The reduction in the value of maintenance grant payments and the accompanying increase in loan, overdraft, and credit facilities, intended to ease students' financial difficulties, have inevitably increased their levels of indebtedness (Mintel International Group, 1995). The resulting heightened pressure on both students and banks seems to have changed their relative roles and given rise to distrust. Now there is a prevalent tendency among students to perceive banks as exhibiting indifference or in some cases even to feel resentment towards them, and students often feel as though they are being viewed as short-term burdens while at university with long-term profit potential when they enter employment (Hartstone 1996). To some observers it may seem that banks conduct themselves as though they do not trust students, viewing them as financially irresponsible, while simultaneously reinforcing financial irresponsibility through the allocation of cash incentives, extensive overdrafts and an accommodating public image. This paper proposes that these two effects lead to the development of 'duplicitous attitudes' in the student–bank relationship in the UK (that is, students and banks behave towards each other in a manner contrary to their beliefs).

The second part of this chapter compares students in the UK and students in France to see whether attitudes towards banks and the student–bank relationship are different in these two cultures. France was chosen because it has no official government-sponsored loans scheme and there is a more 'traditional' approach to the use of credit and the financing of periods of study, with a greater tendency to use family resources, part-time jobs and savings to fund higher education. Consequently the use of bank overdraft and credit card facilities are less common among young people.

Method[1]

Study 1

Four focus groups were conducted, each consisting of six undergraduates from the University of Bath. All 24 participants were final year students, 12 male and 12 female.

A number of topic areas were introduced during the course of the focus groups including the best and worst aspects of banks, personal bank experiences, perception of student vs bank attitudes, and the persuasiveness of bank advertisements.

Study 2

As with Study 1, focus groups were the research tool used to look at the nature of the student–bank relationship, but on this occasion the study was specifically designed to compare the views of students in the UK with those in France.

The UK research involved six focus groups with students from the University of Bath and the University of Exeter. The French study consisted of six focus groups with students from René Descartes University, in Paris. This time, the sample included first year, mid-term and final year students, all aged between 18 and 24, and there was an even gender split. In both France and the UK focus groups were comprised of four to eight participants.

Once again, topic areas were introduced to guide discussion, including the nature of the student–bank relationship, personal bank experiences, and the perception of student vs bank attitudes.

Results[2]

Study 1

Participant comments provided confirmation that students perceive an attitudinal conflict between themselves and the banks, which takes place in several areas of the relationship. The availability of credit was found to have a negative effect on 'financial conscientiousness' (the responsible use of money), and evidence indicated that participants saw an enforced link between being a student and the use of credit, which may have implications for their financial behaviour. Furthermore, the perception of conflicting attitudes between students and banks was strongly reflected in participant notions of financial conscientiousness:

> "It's a contradiction – they're teaching you financial responsibility on the one hand by fining you for going over your [overdraft] limit and giving you the hard line, but at the same time they're going, 'Here, have some more money'."

> "I started off [my university life] not being like that [financially irresponsible], but the more it's available, the more you just spend without thinking about it."

With this in mind, the key themes found within participant comments will be outlined with examples given where appropriate, followed by the exploration of specific themes relating to the student–bank relationship.

Developing negatives

A common theme involved the concern participants had over the way their bank appeared 'uninvolved' and 'corporate like' with regards to student issues, which was a reflection of the discrepancies between the way banks portrayed themselves in the media and students' personal experiences.

Some referred to the detached nature of the relationship between students and banks, and the apparent lack of personal interaction. It was also suggested that banks frequently acted in an unnecessarily austere manner and presented a 'split personality' as illustrated by the following two quotes:

> "One time I was two hundred quid over my [overdraft] limit because I'd been paying on Switch and [using] cashback; and I got this phone call from some Liverpudlian bloke [independent debt collector], threatening to send my card back to the bank or they'd send the police round to take it off me."

> "I imagine my bank as two people … when you want to borrow money it's the young 30 [-year-old], understanding image … [but when] … something goes wrong … it's the 50-year-old treading on your face."

A positive direction

A second group of comments represents a more positive side to the relationship and emphasises potentially good practice on the part of banks in dealing with their student clientele and therefore may be vital in redressing problems with the student–bank relationship. Students were particularly appreciative of banks that empathised with their situation and took an honest approach in their advertising; for example, when talking of a particular bank one participant said:

> "They have respect for me as a customer and understand my needs."

In another case the student felt as though the bank was saying:

> "We don't know you personally and don't claim to, but we're specialists in offering a banking service and isn't that the most important thing we can offer you – help and advice?"

The hidden agenda

The hidden agenda concerns itself with the promotion of credit use, and the financial irresponsibility, or negative financial conscientiousness, seemingly encouraged by banks:

> "If I were to ring up my bank and ask to extend my overdraft by two hundred quid, they'd say, 'Oh, certainly. No problem'. They're too accommodating.... When it comes to the end of the year and you're facing a massive overdraft, you're in trouble. And what do they do to help you out then? They don't realise that ... you have to go through hell trying to pay it off."

Having said this, however, students were equally displeased when banks tried to stop them from borrowing more money as typified by this comment:

> "I went to get my overdraft changed [increased] and they said I had to go and see this woman in town, and it was this woman who basically had a go at everything about my whole life, I had to explain everything about what I spent and where I spent it."

Duplicitous attitudes

Most of the excerpts given so far suggest a dichotomy of fundamental attitudes held by the students and their banks. The lack of 'loyalty' exhibited may be interpreted as a result of the seemingly inherent conflict in the student–bank relationship. One participant comment, for example, illustrates how students and banks might behave towards each other in a way contrary to their beliefs (that is, the duplicitous nature of the student–bank relationship):

> "Banks think: 'Students are an easy target. Although lending them money is a drain in some ways, we make it up with fines. We don't care if they do not like it.' Banks say: 'We care about students. We are

> happy to lend you money at university to make your life easier. We will help you to manage your money, we understand your needs'."

> "Students think: 'I do not care about the bank because I know it does not care about me. I will use and abuse it as much as I can – I'm not fooled.' Students say: 'I am a responsible student – I am in control of my money. If you lend it to me I will use it responsibly'."

Other comments centred on the feelings of distrust students had towards their bank and the lack of loyalty they felt towards them, for example:

> "When you first go in and they're really friendly you think, 'Oh, this is really nice', but when you've been a student for four years, at the end of it you're just like, 'Don't be smug, you're out to get my money, you're giving me as much money as I ask for because you're going to rake it in afterwards'."

> "I'm impartial; I've no burning desire to change bank, but I've got no devout loyalty to my bank.... I might as well be banking with the Royal Bank of Swaziland."

Target accuracy

The final theme to be discussed encompasses the advertising-only themes and the breadth of understanding that participants believed banks had of their target market. It is reflective of key issues in participants' responses to the advertisements, and highlights the gap between images portrayed in the media and the practicalities of the student–bank relationship. Most advertisements were criticised, whether for assuming that students were naive and gullible, for trying too hard to be 'hip and cool', or for overgeneralising about the student population. The following quotes typify a few of these criticisms:

> "Missing the point – disappointing – appealing to people I do not want to be associated with."

> "The one [ad] where he was going [assumes voice of game-show host], 'People do different things to get money, young people, what you need is this card!'. I think [it] takes the piss – really patronising."

"Some weird student. That we all drink snakebite and are into grunge – stereotyping."

Specific themes relating to the student–bank relationship

A number of the themes already outlined had specific significance in relation to the student–bank relationship, and once again there was a particular prevalence of duplicitous attitudes. Participants' perceptions of what 'banks think', their experiences of what 'banks say', and their personal views on what 'students think' and what 'students say' will be considered in turn.

Some of the major themes relating to what 'banks think' were the impersonal nature of the bank's outlook; the distrust that prevails between students and their banks; and the indifference with which students felt they were treated. Examples of participant comments include, "Charge him for anything he does", "Make him trust us" and "We will try to screw this person".

In relation to what 'banks say' there was an emphasis on the caring attitudes conveyed by the bank towards the student. The results suggested a facade adopted by the bank, which was different from their motives. There was also a high degree of similarity in what banks had to say to students, perhaps reflecting the competitive nature of the market, and the issue of 'offers' emerged again. The following are examples of participant comments: "Come and join us and you can get such and such free gift", and "We really want to help you get through university".

When referring to what 'students think' the themes were dominated by a lack of financial conscientiousness, the implications of which sometimes resulted in fear. Examples of participant comments include, "It's a non-realisation of how much I have actually borrowed because everyone around me is in the same position", and "What happens if I can't pay off my overdraft? I haven't actually got a clue what my 'real' financial situation is".

Finally, when considering what 'students say' positive financial conscientiousness was consistent among the majority of comments. It transpired that participants liked to reassure their banks of their financial responsibility whatever state their finances were in. This was linked with the duplicitous nature of the relationship many participants had with their bank. The following are examples of participant comments: "My finances are organised, I can account for all outgoings and have every intention of paying the money back", and "Thank you very much,

I'm very responsible with my money and I should not be any bother to you".

Study 2

This study further developed the findings of Study 1 by providing a comparison between the UK and France, helping to understand national differences in financial conscientiousness and students' attitudes towards banks.

Economic socialisation

A large proportion of UK students were in debt and the majority accepted the legitimate need for the use of credit. Participants mentioned the widespread availability of loans at low interest rates and that taking out a loan was a commonplace activity. Those who initially avoided credit use often accepted it after encountering the 'realities of student life', through a process of socialisation:

> "... in the beginning it was like guilt [being in debt], but then you realise that everyone else is the same, so it's okay." (UK student)

Students came to the point where they considered the use of credit to be not only acceptable, but to be a necessary and integral part of student life:

> "Well, it becomes more accepted. People in their first year come in and they don't want to get into debt but you have to change your attitude because you realise that you're not going to get through, especially as people underestimate a lot of how much they are going to spend at university and they don't realise that people socialise a huge amount." (UK student)

There was an identifiable trend for UK students to become increasingly familiar with and dependent upon borrowing. This socialisation process into the use of credit may have repercussions on leaving university:

> "It's brilliant being in the red, because you can live a little bit above what you should do. You can be in debt for the whole of your life

> and if you earn a certain amount you can live like you're earning a little bit more." (UK student)

In all there were 48 'debt' contributions from the UK participants; 36 of these expressed the need for, or inevitability of, credit use and some displayed a cavalier attitude towards it. There were only 12 statements which clearly showed a preference for either wishing to pay it off as soon as possible on commencing paid employment, or avoiding the use of credit in the first place.

There was a sharp contrast between the UK and French groups. French participants adopted a more cautious attitude towards credit and debt, and getting into any significant debt (over 3,000F/£300) was rare, even the arrangement of relatively small overdraft facilities like these were considered (dramatically) by some to be risk-forming behaviour:

> "I'd compare it to gamblers' fever, getting repeatedly into debt ... [some] are clutched by their financial and social situation and don't manage to make it out because life compels them to need money and they're forced to borrow more money. And there's also the fact that there's often a lack of information, people tend to take several little loans, which cost them much more, and which draw them even more quickly into the vicious circle." (French student)

French students talked like citizens of a nation strongly discouraged from using credit. Unlike UK students, they did not mention their large social expenses and they generally utilised part-time jobs, forms of parental support and savings as alternative means of supporting themselves.

Attitudes towards banks

UK participants expressed a distrust of institutions in general and of banks in particular, which often manifested itself in hostility:

> "I don't trust banks anyway. All they want is your money and ... they've been incredibly unhelpful most of the time." (UK student)

It was also noted that the majority of UK students had more than one account, which may also reflect this cynical attitude:

> "I don't understand this 'you should have one student account and that's it'. They can go take a running jump, they don't say that to people they've got working [in employment]. I play them off one against the other." (UK student)

The ratio of remarks in the UK expressing distrust of institutions, including banks, to those expressing any kind of approval was 30:4. Reasons for this distrust included the 'coercive' quality of the relationship, profit as a motive, and stories of mistakes and misunderstandings, which serve as justification for distrust:

> "The banks are quite happy to coerce you to bank with them, but when it comes down to it they are quite happy to charge you."

> "I have no loyalties to the bank at all."

> "The thing I don't like about [banks] trying to be friendly with people is that ... it's false, because when it comes down to it, it's money and they don't care if you're a student."

There was no comparable level of suspicion in the French groups. They recognised that banks were 'in business', which did not condemn them, and that they offered a valuable service:

> "The overdraft is a service the bank renders, even if it takes advantage of it, it is still a service. But to be allowed an overdraft of 3,000F for 15 days, without owing anything to the bank if you pay it back in due time, is great because it permits you to manage your account with much more flexibility.... You will have an overdraft, but it's not serious because you will be able to pay it off."

French students also took their banks more seriously, showing respect and sometimes fear (unlike the confident UK attitude typified by the remark, "If they don't give me what I want I'll take my overdraft elsewhere"):

> "... it would scare me to get into debt in an extreme way. I am scared of ... seeing my credit card taken away. Without a credit card, without a cheque book, you are almost excluded from society; we live in a system where everything is controlled by money. I am afraid to see myself without means of payment and cast out from

society. Not rejected, but in a sense ... because everything is monitored by the money system."

Conclusion

Results of the study found positive confirmation for the perceived existence of duplicitous attitudes in the student–bank relationship in the UK. Students overwhelmingly viewed banks as being guilty of acting contrary to their beliefs, while revealing that they themselves acted in a duplicitous manner towards their bank. This duplicity was mirrored in students' interpretations of the images banks conveyed through advertising, suggesting a possible mismanagement of resources both in advertising and the special conditions that banks offer students. It might be argued that banks aim to keep student custom in the hope of reaping returns when students embark on their working careers, but the UK students in this study appeared unwilling to pledge their loyalty. There was also evidence that students who expressed plans to stay with their banks were doing so out of apathy or because 'all banks are the same' rather than through any positive feelings towards their bank; a finding that is also common among the UK population as a whole (for example, Dick and Basu, 1994).

The findings imply that 'negative financial conscientiousness' in the relationship might be a circular phenomenon. Students believe banks stereotype them as financially irresponsible, while simultaneously offering financial responsibility through extensive credit facilities[3]. Meanwhile, students are enticed by easily available credit facilities and feel justified in acting irresponsibly because everyone is in the 'same boat' and their bank does little to discourage them.

There was some consensus among participants that the accommodating nature of banks was unethical and that they were taking advantage of students in offering extensive credit. In concern over the encouragement of negative financial conscientiousness one participant protested that banks are supposed to know, suggesting that the eagerness to utilise credit is coupled with an unwillingness to accept financial responsibility.

On the surface it may appear that students find themselves confronted with a financial conundrum. On the one hand they are keen to prove that they are financially responsible and independent, while simultaneously they are tempted by reckless urges induced by the availability of credit facilities (reminiscent of the behavioural life-cycle hypothesis proposed by Shefrin and Thaler, 1988). The study, however, found that the kind of financial conscientiousness exhibited by students towards their bank was often a 'mask' to match the bank's facade of being a caring 'financial friend'. These UK findings reveal the true extent of the problem of the perceptions of contradicting 'private' and 'public' attitudes and persona (duplicitous attitudes).

When UK students were compared to French students, the UK experience was found to include an additional stage of economic socialisation that does not occur in France, starting on arrival at university. As first years they often preferred to avoid the use of credit, particularly uncontrolled borrowing (for example, deferred credit card repayment). However, there were clearly norms that evolved (usually within the first year): an expectation developed that some debt would be built up over the years of study, and it became accepted that a fair proportion of this spending would be on social activity. In France, by contrast, owing money to banks was seen as something to be actively avoided, regardless of year of study.

Finally, economic attitudes demonstrated by students in the UK were also quite distinct from those exhibited by students in France. Student comments in the UK culminated in a fairly undifferentiated hostility towards financial institutions and market relations in general, with statements expressing distrust of institutions to those expressing approval (of banks in particular) being in the ratio of 6:1. In France, by comparison, there was greater respect for financial institutions, and the recognition of banks as service providers for which they were entitled to profits in some form.

Notes

[1] More detailed information concerning the research methods is included in Appendix A.

[2] All scripts were transcribed independently by the authors prior to the identification of any common themes in the data set, and all participant comments are representative of these prevalent issues.

[3] It should be noted that these participant perceptions might not be wholly accurate. Scott and Lewis (2000a) conducted pilot interviews with two student managers and found they did not stereotype students on any personal level, but differentiated them from the rest of the population according to their

rather unusual circumstances (their first time away from home coupled with a sudden influx of money). Furthermore, the student managers acknowledged that it would be irresponsible for banks to hand out large overdrafts to students without good reason.

Part IV: Summing up

EIGHT

Theoretical and policy implications

Adrian J. Scott, Alan Lewis and Stephen E.G. Lea

In six empirical chapters evidence has been presented on money management skills, student attitudes towards credit and debt, the influence of the student loan scheme on well-being, and the relationship students have with their banks. The studies differ in size and methodology: some relied on relatively small numbers presenting mostly qualitative information from focus groups and interviews; others employed questionnaires, had a larger number of participants, and quantitative analysis was apt. None of these studies on their own allow us to draw widespread conclusions with any great confidence. Taken together, and where there are consistencies, however, some tentative generalisations are justified. The first section below outlines these consistent results across studies.

As with any research project there will also be inconsistent patterns; these will be discussed under the subtitle 'Inconsistencies and conundrums'. The following sections debate, in turn, the relevance of these findings for theory (especially work in economic psychology), and for policy. Recommendations for future research are then outlined and a brief conclusion comprises the finale.

Consistencies and tentative generalisations

When UK students consider going to university, and when they first arrive, the use of credit is seen as a bad thing, but during an undergraduate's career borrowing becomes a necessity and attitudes towards credit and debt soften. Associated with this acceptance is a growing awareness of the size of the final amount they will have to repay, a figure which is grossly underestimated in the early days of this tacit period of 'financial education' and 'economic socialisation'. At the start, the student loan is not viewed as a 'debt', but further down the road it clearly is, suggesting that the size of the loan is important in determining how it is perceived. This is particularly significant, as having what are seen as 'excessive' debts is a source of considerable anxiety among some students.

Students are generally poor money managers and they know this themselves. For some, there seems little point in budgeting given the inevitability of at least some debt. For others (and a disproportionate number are women) there is some attempt at stemming the tide but even here there is a feeling that ultimately the burden will be excessive. Men are more likely to have tolerant attitudes towards credit and debt and to spend 'irresponsibly', especially on alcohol and social activities, even as the amount they owe rises. This kind of spending seems to be a characteristic of the UK student culture as it is unusual in both Italy and France. Also, unlike in France, there is an antipathy towards banks and financial institutions among UK undergraduates.

Another consistent result from the studies reported here is that there are different types of student money management, and that some students manage their finances better than others, even when their objective circumstances are the same. Nonetheless, the widespread nature of student money difficulties, and the worries they bring in their train, is a depressing reality.

Inconsistencies and conundrums

Every trend has its exceptions, of course. Evidence has been reported that attitudes towards credit and debt become more tolerant as the amount borrowed increases: that attitudes adapt to changing financial circumstances. Yet it seems that attitudes towards credit and debt become less tolerant after graduation as the borrowings start to be repaid. Superficially, this is at odds with the chapters in this book that have argued that the 'economic socialisation' during this period may have longer-term, potentially harmful, effects by encouraging cavalier attitudes towards credit and debt. This particular circle can be easily squared, however. Although it is true that attitudes towards credit and debt become less tolerant after graduation, this is also a reflection of a change in financial circumstances – once in employment, borrowing is no longer a necessity. Furthermore, the distaste for credit and debt does not return to the levels found among prospective undergraduates, suggesting that the experience of student debt does leave an 'attitudinal residue'.

Some students in debt are anxious about it, some are apt to say 'to hell with it, let's party!', and some may even adopt both of these attitudes at once. We have already seen that men are more likely to take a 'devil-may-care' attitude and women are more likely to budget and be anxious. Both of these can be seen as a kind of coping strategy, which may be linked to perceived locus of control. The problem is that neither an external nor an internal locus of control alone may be healthy. In the first case, the use of credit may get out of hand, and in the second, although the effort is praiseworthy, the belief that one can be left with an excessive burden remains, as does the associated anxiety and depression.

Implications for economic psychology

This part is really a continuation of the 'Inconsistencies and conundrums' section above, as the empirical studies have produced mixed evidence for and against the life-cycle hypothesis (LCH), compared to the behavioural life-cycle hypothesis (BLCH). In most life-cycle models (for example, Ando and Modigliani, 1963) the economic actor is envisaged as calculating lifetime income and the varying expenditure patterns required over time, and then behaving rationally. Such an actor would view student loans both as an investment in their human capital resulting in above-average salaries in the future, and as 'cheap money'[1]. Consequently, rational economic man would treat a student loan favourably as 'credit', rather than negatively as 'debt'.

From the studies reported in this book, however, it is rare for students to view the loan scheme as a favourable form of credit. As they progress through their degree, and the amount they owe to the Student Loans Company increases, it becomes viewed and treated more negatively, like a 'debt'. In the UK it is more often than not the students from less wealthy families who owe the most. In Italy, by comparison, it is typically the wealthier students who borrow money and although they have no organised student loan scheme, there is a choice. Within this context, the money borrowed is more likely to be viewed favourably as 'credit' than negatively as 'debt'. Furthermore, contrary to the LCH, owing money is far from an emotionally neutral experience and the act of being in 'debt' (especially if this is viewed as being an excessive amount) causes many students concern and anxiety.

In contrast to the LCH, the BLCH (Shefrin and Thaler, 1988) accepts that there is a rational 'planner' in us all, but that there is also a more impulsive 'doer', who is rather short-sighted, wanting to live now, not later. The male students in this book certainly appear to be suffering from a degree of short-sightedness: as their levels of debt increase they largely give up budgeting but carry on drinking. Even when forced to look into the future they tend to overestimate their potential incomes, which is far from the complete knowledge assumption of the rational economic man paradigm. Furthermore, beliefs or attitudes corresponding to the LCH, or anything similar, have hardly ever been articulated in any of the focus groups or interviews in this book. The short-sighted 'doer' of the BLCH is, however, on this evidence, a realistic description of the contemporary student in debt – especially the male student.

But wait a minute. Perhaps women are right to worry more, budget more, and be less tolerant of credit and debt as their future lifetime incomes are likely to be lower than those of men; perhaps men are exhibiting 'affordable irresponsibility'. There may be bravado in overestimating future income and in today's clubbing and boozing – but at some level there is a calculation, if only an implicit one, that things will turn out all right. After all, male graduates might have larger loans but they worry less and are able to pay them off more quickly.

A great deal of research in economic psychology, and psychology generally, is based on self-report studies – what people have to say about themselves, the accounts they give of their own thinking, attitudes and behaviour – but there are other ways of modelling behaviour and the 'as if' assumptions of the LCH are one. If the LCH fits the facts it may still have validity even though it might not be the story we wish to tell. We do not deny that the 'objective' facts, such as the size of loans, how quickly they are repaid, financial differences between men and women, and the wealth of their families, matter a great deal in any comprehensive analysis. But so do the 'subjective' experiences and the internal worlds of students that have been included in this book. After all, when considering the well-being of students it is not just the amount owed that matters, but the interpretation of this and whether it is viewed as manageable or excessive.

Implications for policy[2]

This book has not been dedicated to an analysis of the effect of the loan scheme on recruitment, wastage rates or the changing demographics of the student population. The research is, however, important in the context of rising student debt, where levels are set to rise further still. Changes in the government financing of higher education have resulted in an increase in the number of UK students at university. The costs borne by undergraduates, their families and guardians are not solely financial; the high levels of debt cause anxiety and academic performance can suffer, either directly or from the extra paid work taken on by students worried about being in debt[3].

The research included in this book has two broadly defined implications for policy: the student loan scheme should not simply be viewed as a substitute for the grant system, and if the present system of funding is to remain, there needs to be some education regarding money management and the interpretation of student debt. These will be considered in turn.

First, the replacement of the non-repayable grant-based system by the repayable loan-based one should not be considered straightforward because student debt has a negative effect on students' well-being. David Blunkett, the Education and Employment Secretary, defended the introduction of student loans on the grounds that they do not penalise the student at the point of entry, but ask for a contribution at the point of reward (cited in Sherman, 1998). If it is assumed that students are self-interested utility maximisers this statement is justified: undergraduates will view their student loan borrowings in terms of their life-cycle and subsequently treat it as an investment in their human capital, which will lead to above-average incomes in the future. The evidence presented in this book, however, suggests that although the borrowing behaviour of students fits into the general framework of the LCH, it is unable to account for the associated feelings of discomfort, anxiety and depression. We would argue that in order to address these issues a more psychological approach to policy making such as the BLCH is needed in the future.

Second, if student loans are to remain the principal source of finance for poorer students, some formal education regarding money management and the interpretation of student debt is needed. What is more, the provision of this 'knowledge, aptitude and skill base' young people need has to start in schools to be effective, otherwise the opportunity to reach everyone equally is lost (Davies, 2001). As Leonard (1995) pointed out, recent changes to policy were not only driven by financial considerations but also by the belief among policy makers that students were becoming part of a 'dependency culture', a dependency that could be broken by the loan scheme. The presented research, however, suggests that instead of encouraging financial responsibility and removing this 'dependency culture', a 'borrowing culture' is being unwittingly put in its place.

The government, the banks and financial institutions may be giving out the wrong signals: that borrowing is 'cool'. Students feel manipulated, and there is an increased cynicism towards banks and financial institutions; a finding that is not evident in France where student borrowing is less common. Undergraduates are financially naive and many do not understand how credit works: the real size of the repayments they face only dawns on them shortly before graduation or even afterwards. Furthermore, the loan scheme also means that undergraduates have little or no financial independence from their parents while at university and for some years afterwards.

One possible way of improving the situation for future students, without major reform, would be to better prepare them for the university experience. As Boddington and Kemp (1999) have argued, students need to gain a realistic notion of how much they will be likely to owe when they graduate and how to use credit effectively before they start to view it negatively as debt[4]. Although there is some 'personal finance education' (PFE) in schools, the majority of people believe school leavers are 'ill-equipped for financial independence', and economic ignorance is rife (Lewis and Scott, 2000; Ewels et al, 1998; Lewis and van Venrooij, 1995; Ranyard and Craig, 1993). According to a MORI poll for the Qualifications and Curriculum Authority, most children aged between 11 and 16 prioritised learning about 'money skills' when asked what they most wanted to learn in preparation for adult life, which was ahead of sex education (Financial Services Authority, 2001). PFE is currently given via a number of formally assessed courses (for example, maths, business studies, economics) or forms part of 'personal, social and health education' which is taught alongside the national curriculum (PSHE/ct, 2000). But teachers report that non-statutory aspects of education are often neglected (Knights, a) and the lessons offered at present are frequently judged to be irrelevant to the pupils' experiences (Ewels et al, 1998).

Blanket calls for more education and greater consumer protection, in this case for rather naive credit users, are frequent. Certainly, the loan scheme is a crash course in economic socialisation resulting in a rude awakening, but there must be a better way. The learning process needs to be made interesting and relevant to the individual needs (Knights, a); perhaps students would take more notice if such courses were part of their curriculum and contextualised as skills for making students better off. PFE would also benefit from using an integrated approach to teaching, incorporating practical learning and formal education (Lewis and Scott, 2000). One of the greatest problems relating to the improvement of PFE is how to make it relevant while avoiding the sensitive issues that surround it; children come from very different social backgrounds with varied experiences of handling money (Davies, 2001; Ewels et al, 1998). A number of new resources aimed at building upon personal finance issues raised in the primary school curriculum were discussed at the recent Annual Education Conference, including a new Channel Four series aimed at 11 to 16-year-olds and a web-based resource for pupils over the age of 14 (Financial Services Agency, 2001). Prissiness should be avoided, and courses, both before undergraduates arrive at university and afterwards, should address the reality that students in the UK spend a lot of money on social activities. In some of the literature given to school pupils this type of expenditure is not mentioned at all. If intending students perceive the absurdity of this, they are unlikely to take such literature seriously, and if they do not, they will end up with ineffective views and strategies on budgeting. Advice on reducing expenditure on 'entertainment' will be less effective than advice on methods of increasing income and using credit to the best effect.

Education relating to the levels of debt they are likely to have, however, is not enough on its own. Evidence has been presented showing that even students who feel they have good money management skills can still feel despondent because of the perceived excessive burden they face. It is inevitable that the majority of students are going to incur some debt while at university, so there needs to be some education focusing on the interpretation of student debt. While it is not desirable to encourage the use of credit it is important that those forced to incur debt do not feel anxious or depressed as a result.

Future research

Important work needs to be done with financial statistics tracing the size of loans, repayments and the possible influences of the loan scheme on future credit use. Not least one would want to trace the influence on employment and salaries sought and the possible effects on family life: would it be 'rational' for females to start a family and postpone loan repayments; or would the need to repay mean the postponement of child rearing, perhaps forever? At the same time it is imperative to trace the more subjective elements of a research agenda in economic psychology. How do attitudes towards credit and debt change or develop after university? Was the experience of the student loan scheme beneficial or detrimental in the long term? Will students who enrol in university after the abolition of the maintenance grant and the introduction of tuition fees come to see their borrowings as an 'investment' in their future earning potential[5]?

It will no longer do to rely on the perceptions of students alone when exploring the views of the 'consumers'. The loan scheme has meant that parents and guardians have been increasingly involved. Financial arrangements can be complex, with parents providing private loans and 'gifts' over long periods. Research in the context of the power of language and competing political claims also needs to be conducted: does the loan scheme reduce 'dependency on the state', increase 'financial responsibility and independence', and educate young people in the effective use of credit, or does it create a 'borrowing culture', and a deep wariness of financial institutions and 'free' market forces?

The broader picture is one that takes into account culture, political-economic history and time. Cultural comparisons reveal that respect for banks and other financial institutions has fallen in the UK, but this cannot be blamed on the increased use of credit, including the loan scheme; different cultures have varying political-economic histories and expectations.

Conclusion

This book has reported on nine previously unpublished empirical studies examining different aspects of student debt in the UK. The cross-cultural comparisons with Italy and France have shown that the experiences of students in the UK are unique. The main theme running throughout the book is that student debt, particularly the student loan scheme, is having a negative effect on the well-being of students. In relation to theory this finding suggests that the LCH or similar economic models are of little use when considering student health, and that a more psychological model, such as the BLCH, is called upon to address this issue. When looking at policy, it is apparent that the student loan scheme has helped address the financial shortfalls of the grant system but this has come at a cost to the student and their families.

The findings of this book have two main implications for policy. Firstly, it should be acknowledged that the student loan scheme is not a simple substitute for the grant system as there are consequences for student well-being. Assumptions about 'rational economic man' can often be misplaced and policy makers should be made aware of the psychological realities of economic decision making as well as the influence of early experience on future behaviour. Finally, if the present system of funding is to remain, PFE must be improved so that school pupils leave secondary education with the basic financial skills necessary for financial independence.

Notes

[1] It should be noted that a feature of the government loan scheme at this time was its availability to all students, including the better-off who were not previously in receipt of grants. Consequently, if an individual was wealthy enough not to need a student loan it would still be worthwhile taking it and investing it elsewhere, although very few students were in this somewhat enviable position.

[2] The policy implications outlined in this book consider PFE within the context of preparing students for the financial pressures of university and as a consequence exclude the wider issue of social exclusion. It has been pointed out that PFE may actually strengthen the gap between the middle class and the poor, and that attention needs to be given to the impact of PFE on less affluent groups (see Knights, b).

[3] Nearly two thirds of full-time students work during the academic year and as many as 82% work during the summer vacation (Callender and Kemp, 2000); according to the UNITE/MORI (2001) report, the majority of students who work during term time agree that it adversely affects their university studies.

[4] Scott and Lewis (2000b) conducted a pilot interview with a student money adviser at the University of Bath and were told that university money advisers nationwide now introduce themselves to new undergraduates during induction week, but very few students seek advice about money management before they get into financial difficulties.

[5] The UNITE/MORI (2001) report found that 84% of students in their sample agreed that the money they are spending on their education is a good investment in their future; but it did not consider students' interpretations of the 'debt' itself.

References

Ando, A. and Modigliani, F. (1963) 'The life cycle hypothesis of saving: aggregate implications and tests', *American Economic Review*, vol 53, no 1, pp 55-84.

Ashley, P. (1983) *The money problems of the poor: A literature review*, London: Heinemann Educational Books Limited.

Baines and Ernst (2001) *Key facts*, Manchester: Weber Shandwick, 19 February.

Barclays News Release (2000) 'Graduate debt soars as Barclays launches new package designed to ease financial pressure', 18 April.

Barr, N. (1993) *The economics of the welfare state* (2nd edn), Oxford: Oxford University Press.

Becker, G.S. (1974) *Human capital* (2nd edn), Chicago, IL: University of Chicago Press.

Bellamy, G.W. (1994) *The student money matters project*, Exeter: University of Exeter and National Westminster Bank.

Bem, D.J. (1972) 'Self-perception theory', in L. Berkowitz (ed) *Advances in experimental social psychology*, vol 6, New York, NY: Academic Press, pp 1-62.

Boddington, L. and Kemp, S. (1999) 'Student debt, attitudes towards debt, impulsive buying, and financial management', *New Zealand Journal of Psychology*, vol 28, no 2, pp 89-93.

Callender, C. and Kemp, M. (2000) *Changing student finances: Income, expenditure and the take-up of student loans among full- and part-time higher education students in 1998/99* (www.dfee.gov.uk/research/).

Callender, C. and Kempson, E. (1996) *Student finances: Income, expenditure and take up of student loans*, London: Policy Studies Institute.

Click, R.W. (1996) 'Contrarian macparity', *Economics Letters*, vol 53, no 2, pp 209-12.

Davies, E. and Lea, S.E.G. (1995) 'Student attitudes to student debt', *Journal of Economic Psychology*, vol 16, no 4, pp 663-79.

Davies, H. (2001) FSA second education conference speech, 8 March (www.fsa.org.uk/pubs/speeches/sp74.html).

DfEE (Department for Education and Employment) (1998) *Student loans: Guidance on terms and conditions*, Glasgow: Department for Education and Employment.

Dick, A. and Basu, K. (1994) 'Customer loyalty: toward an integrated framework', *Journal of the Academy of Marketing Science*, vol 22, no 2, pp 99-113.

Education Training Youth, Eurydice and Eurostat (1997) *Key data on education in the European Union*, Luxembourg: Office for Official Publications of the European Communities.

Ewels, J., Knights, D., McLean, C. and Odih, P. (1998) *'Growing up' with personal finance education: Young people's perceptions*, Nottingham: Nottingham University Business School.

Feinberg, R.A. (1986) 'Credit cards as spending facilitating stimuli: a conditioning interpretation', *Journal of Consumer Research*, vol 13, no 3, pp 348-56.

Festinger, L. (1954) 'A theory of social comparison processes', *Human Relations*, vol 7, pp 117-40.

Festinger, L. (1957) *A theory of cognitive dissonance theory*, Stanford, CA: Stanford University Press.

Financial Services Authority (2001) FSA hosts second annual education conference press release, 8 March (www.fsa.gov.uk/pubs/press/2001/028.html).

Friedman, M. (1957) *A theory of the consumption function*, Princeton, NJ: Princeton University Press.

Furnham, A. (1986) 'Economic locus of control', *Human Relations*, vol 39, no 1, pp 29-43.

Garson, G.D., *PA 765 Statnotes: An online textbook* (www2.chass.ncsu.edu/garson/pa765/statnote.htm).

Glennerster, H. (1993) 'The economics of education: changing fortunes', in N. Barr and D. Whynes (eds) *Current issues in economics of welfare*, London: Macmillan, pp 176-99.

Hartstone, M. (1996) *Mind and mood (FCB)*, London: Central.

Hesketh, A.J. (1999) 'Towards an economic sociology of the student financial experience of higher education', *Journal of Education Policy*, vol 14, no 4, pp 385-410.

Hills, A. (1997) 'Unit handbook: analysis of variance and correlational designs using SPSS for Windows', unpublished manuscript, Edith Cowan University.

International Labour Office (1968) *International standard classification of occupations* (revised edn), Geneva: International Labour Office.

Johnes, G. (1994) 'The determinants of student loan take-up in the United Kingdom', *Applied Economics*, vol 26, no 10, pp 999-1005.

Katona, G. (1964) *The mass consumption society*, New York, NY: McGraw-Hill.

Katona, G. (1975) *Psychological economics*, New York, NY: Elsevier.

Kempson, E., Bryson, A. and Rowlingson, K. (1994) *Hard times: How poor families make ends meet*, London: Policy Studies Institute.

Knights, D. (a) 'Educating the public in financial services: appendices' (www.keele.ac.uk/depts/mn/staff/dk.html).

Knights, D. (b) 'Educating the public in financial services: a summary' (www.keele.ac.uk/depts/mn/staff/dkhome/bpr/Educatingsummary.html).

Le Grand, J. (1997) 'Knights, knaves or pawns? Human behaviour and social policy', *Journal of Social Policy: The journal of the social policy administration*, vol 26, part 2, pp 149-69.

Lea, S.E.G. (1994) 'Rationality: the formalist view', in W. Güth and Brandstätter (eds) *Essays in economic psychology*, Berlin: Springer-Verlag, pp 71-89.

Lea, S.E.G. (1999) 'Credit, debt and problem debt', in P.E. Earl and S. Kemp (eds) *The Elgar companion to consumer research and economic psychology*, Cheltenham: Edward Elgar, pp 139-43.

Lea, S.E.G., Tarpy, R.M. and Webley, P. (1987) *The individual in the economy*, Cambridge: Cambridge University Press.

Lea, S.E.G., Webley, P. and Levine, R.M. (1993) 'The economic psychology of consumer debt', *Journal of Economic Psychology*, vol 14, no 1, pp 85-119.

Lea, S.E.G, Webley, P. and Walker, C.M. (1995) 'Psychological factors in consumer debt: money management, economic socialisation and credit use', *Journal of Economic Psychology*, vol 16, no 4, pp 681-701.

Leonard, M. (1995) 'Labouring to learn: students' debt and term time employment in Belfast', *Higher Education Quarterly*, vol 49, no 3, pp 229-47, July.

Lewis, A. and Scott, A.J. (1999) 'Economic knowledge and awareness among adolescents', unpublished manuscript, University of Bath.

Lewis, A. and Scott, A.J. (2000) 'The economic awareness, knowledge and pocket money practices of a sample of UK adolescents: a study of economic socialisation and economic psychology', *Children's Social and Economics Education: An International Journal*, vol 4, no 1, pp 34-46.

Lewis, A. and van Venrooij, M. (1995) 'A note on the perceptions of loan duration and repayment', *Journal of Economic Psychology*, vol 16, no 1, pp 161-8.

Lewis, A., Sandford, C. and Thompson, N. (1980) *Grants or loans?*, London: The Institute of Economic Affairs.

Lim, V.K.G. and Teo, T.S.H. (1997) 'Sex, money and financial hardship: an empirical study of attitudes towards money among undergraduates in Singapore', *Journal of Economic Psychology*, vol 18, no 4, pp 369-86.

Livingstone, S.M. and Lunt, P.K. (1992) 'Predicting personal debt and debt repayment: psychological, social and economic determinants', *Journal of Economic Psychology*, vol 13, no 1, pp 111-34.

McCarthy, P. and Humphrey, R. (1995) 'Debt: the reality of student life', *Higher Education Quarterly*, vol 49, no 1, pp 78-86, January.

Mintel International Group (1995) 'Marketing financial services to children and students', *Personal Finance Intelligence*, vol 2, London: Mintel International Group.

Modigliani, F. and Brumberg, R. (1954) 'Utility analysis and the consumption function: an interpretation of cross-section data', in K.K. Kurihara (ed) *Post-Keynesian economics*, New Brunswick, NJ: Rutgers University Press.

O'Leary, J. (1997) 'Labour accused of hitting poor with tuition fees for students' (www.times-archive.co.uk/cgi-bin/BackIssue).

Ong, L.L. (1997) 'Burgernomics: the economics of the Big Mac standard', *Journal of International Money and Finance*, vol 16, no 6, pp 865-78.

Prince, M. (1993) 'Women, men, and money styles', *Journal of Economic Psychology*, vol 14, no 1, pp 175-82.

PSHE/ct (2000) *Personal, social and health education and citizenship at Key Stages 1 and 2: Initial guidance for schools*, London: Qualifications and Curriculum Authority Publications.

Ranyard, R. and Craig, G. (1993) 'Estimating the duration of a flexible loan: the effect of supplementary information', *Journal of Economic Psychology*, vol 14, no 2, pp 317-35.

Roberts, R., Golding, J. and Towell, T. (1998) 'Student finance and mental health', *The Psychologist*, vol 11, no 10, pp 489-91.

Sarason, I.G., Johnson, J.H. and Siegel, J.M. (1978) 'Assessing the impact of life changes: development of the life experience survey', *Journal of Consulting and Clinical Psychology*, vol 46, no 5, pp 932-46.

Scitovsky, T. (1976) *The joyless economy*, Oxford: Oxford University Press.

Scott, A.J. and Lewis, A. (2000a) 'Student debt: the bank's perspective', unpublished manuscript, University of Bath.

Scott, A.J. and Lewis, A. (2000b) 'Student money matters', unpublished manuscript, University of Bath.

Seaward, H.G.W. and Kemp, S. (2000) 'Optimism bias and student debt', *New Zealand Journal of Psychology*, vol 29, no 1, pp 17-19.

Shefrin, H. and Thaler, R.H. (1988) 'The behavioural life-cycle hypothesis', *Economic Enquiry*, vol 26, no 4, pp 609-43.

Sherman, J. (1998) 'Blunkett sets cap on tuition fees to avert a revolt' (www.times-archive.co.uk/cgi-bin/BackIssue).

Statistical First Release 38 (2000, April 28) *Student enrolments on higher education courses at publicly funded higher education institutions in the United Kingdom for the academic year 1999/2000* (www.hesa.ac.uk/Press/sfr38/sfr38.htm).

StatSoft, Inc. (2001) *Electronic statistics textbook*, Tulsa, OK: StatSoft.

Student Finance Office (1996) *A student budget plan*, Bath: University of Bath.

Sullivan, T.E., Warren, E. and Westbrook, J.L. (1989) *As we forgive our debtors*, New York, NY: Oxford University Press.

Talik, J.B.G. (1999) 'Student loans as the answer to lack of resources for higher education', *Economic and Political Weekly*, vol 19, nos 1-2, p 19.

Thaler, R.H. (1992) *The winner's curse: Paradoxes and anomalies of economic life*, Princetown, NJ: Princetown University Press.

Tokunaga, H. (1993) 'The use and abuse of consumer credit: application of psychological theory and research', *Journal of Economic Psychology*, vol 14, no 2, pp 285-316.

UCLA, Academic Technology Services (2000, 6 April) (www.ats.ucla.edu/stat/spss/faq/alpha.html).

UNITE/MORI (2001) *Student living report*, Bristol: MORI.

Varga, J. (1996) 'On tuition fees and student loans in higher education', *Acta Oeconomica*, vol 48, nos 3-4, pp 297-310.

Vingilis, E., Wade, T.J. and Adlaf, E. (1998) 'What factors predict student self-rated physical health?', *Journal of Adolescence*, vol 21, no 1, pp 83-97.

Walker, C.M. (1997) 'The psychology of debt in the 1990s', upublished PhD thesis, University of Exeter.

Walker, C.M., Lea, S.E.G. and Webley, P. (1992) 'An interview study of the origins of problem debt', Paper read at the 17th conference of the International Association for Research in Economic Psychology, vol 1, pp 118-23.

Warwick-Ching, L. (2001) 'Under-26s in debt', *Financial Times*, 3 May (www.news.ft.com/ft/gx.cgi/ftc?pagename=View&c=Article&cid=FT4RR30CAM&live=true&tagid=YYY9BSINKTM&useoverridetemplate=IXLZHNNP94C#).

Webley, P., Burgoyne, C.B., Lea, S.E.G. and Young, B.M. (2001) *The economic psychology of everyday life*, Hove: Psychology Press.

Webley, P., Lea, S.E.G. and Walker, C.M. (1993) 'Debt, borrowing and saving', Paper read at the 18th conference of the International Association for Research in Economic Psychology, vol 2, pp 297-306.

West, E.G. (1994) 'Britain's student loan system in world perspective: a critique', *Current Controversies*, no 9, pp 9-41.

Winnett, A. and Lewis, A. (1995) 'Household accounts, mental accounts and savings behaviour: some old economics rediscovered?', *Journal of Economic Psychology*, vol 16, no 3, pp 432-48.

Zigmond, A.S. and Snaith, R.P. (1983) 'The hospital anxiety and depression scale', *Acta Psychiatrica Scandinavia*, vol 67, pp 361-70.

Appendix A: Research methods

Where possible, this appendix will provide greater detail of the methods used by the researchers included in this book.

Chapter Two
More money than sense? Investigating student money management

Study 1

The research of Mandy Morgan utilised two research procedures: focus groups and a questionnaire survey. The two focus groups were used to yield qualitative data, designed to identify differences in the money management styles of male and female students. The data generated from the focus groups were then used to produce the questionnaire.

The focus groups were conducted at the participants' convenience and both were conducted in the informal setting of the researcher's home. A hundred questionnaires were administered during lectures over a two-week period; all were returned.

Study 2

The study of Caroline Roberts also used two research methods: individual interviews and a questionnaire survey. The open interview study was designed to give an insight into money management so that a more structured questionnaire could be constructed. The questionnaire survey, therefore, investigated the key elements of student money management revealed by the interviews.

All interviews were conducted individually and in private. First year participants for the questionnaire survey were recruited from halls of residences and final year students through members of the Psychology

Department. All undergraduates were approached individually and the researcher was available for most of the participants to resolve any problems relating to the completion of the questionnaire. The final questionnaire was given to 100 undergraduates; 90 were completed and returned, representing a response rate of 90%.

Study 3

The questionnaire of Paul Powdrill was designed following a review of the relevant literature and informal discussions with people regarding their money management.

Students were approached during their off-duty periods in the coffee bar areas of the university. No time limit was placed on the completion of the questionnaire and the researcher was available to offer assistance. Most questionnaires were fully completed and all 100 were used in the statistical analysis.

Chapter Three
Student debt: expecting it, spending it and regretting it

Each of the three samples involved a different recruitment strategy because of their varied locations. All questionnaires were completed confidentially.

The prospective student sample

Thirty-six sixth form (Year 12) tutors in the South West region were asked to be involved in the research. It was ensured that the schools constituted a representative sample in terms of location, type and size. The completion of questionnaires was achieved via a mixture of school visits and postal correspondence. Of the 800 questionnaires distributed, 659 were returned, representing a response rate of 82%.

Current student sample

University students were approached directly because of their convenient location. Every part of the main campus, from halls of residence to recreational areas and academic buildings, was visited to ensure that a representative sample of students from the University of Exeter was obtained. Of the 2,000 questionnaires distributed 1,318 were returned, of which 1,129 were completed in sufficient detail to be used in statistical analysis, giving an overall response rate of 66% and a usable one of 56%.

The former student sample

The ex-student sample could only be obtained via direct mailing. Printed address labels for graduates of the University of Exeter who left after the introduction of student loans were obtained from the University Alumni Office. Unfortunately, only 54 of the 250 questionnaires delivered were returned, representing a response rate of 22%.

Chapter Four
Student loans: development of a new dependency culture?

Questionnaires were distributed, with the assistance of the Graduate Relations Office, to 500 ex-students (from a total of 1,629) who graduated from the University of Bath in 1997. This graduate year group was chosen because they had attended university after the introduction of student loans, had been away from university for 16 months and were likely to have accurate personal details.

The questionnaires were distributed during November 1998 and 188 completed questionnaires were returned giving an overall response rate of 38%.

Chapter Five
The psychological effects of student debt

Study 1

A large-scale survey of prospective direct entry students who had been made conditional and unconditional offers by the University of Manchester was conducted. Of the 1,200 questionnaires distributed 612 were returned, representing a response rate of 51%.

Study 2

Students were canvassed during their off-duty moments at the University of Manchester and a total of 259 completed questionnaires were collected. Of these, 223 were from students aged 23 or less and counted as direct entry students. The 36 remaining questionnaires from students deemed 'mature' were omitted from the statistical analysis, as they were too small a group to support reliable, separate, analysis.

Study 3

An extensive questionnaire was administered to students from three faculties at the University of Manchester. Unfortunately, only 223 of the 679 questionnaires distributed were returned, representing a response rate of 33%. Of these, 199 were aged 20 or less when they entered university and counted as direct entry students. The 24 questionnaires from 'mature' students were again omitted from the analysis, as they were too small a group to support reliable, separate, statistical analysis.

Chapter Six
Student attitudes towards credit and debt: a cross-national study between Italy and the UK

Questionnaire surveys were conducted over two-week periods in each country; for the Italian sample this was during December 1998 and for the UK sample this was during January 1999. Back-translation was used in order to check that the Italian version of the questionnaire was as similar to the English original as possible.

In Italy, students were approached to complete the questionnaire in 'university rooms' where they usually study. In the UK by comparison they were approached either in the library or in the café bar.

Chapter Seven
Are students serious bankers? The nature of the student–bank relationship in the UK and France

Study 1

The exploratory nature of the topic required a qualitative research design and focus groups were seen as the ideal medium. Participants were selected on an acquaintance basis, although as broad a sample as possible was aimed for. The focus groups were conducted in an informal environment and were no longer than two hours.

Study 2

Focus groups were again utilised as the best way of facilitating an interactive discussion and providing a rich data set. In this study, however, a larger sample was used, participants were approached personally and £10 was offered (or the equivalent in French francs) to undergraduates who agreed to take part in the focus groups. Again, the groups were conducted in an informal setting and lasted no more than two hours.

Appendix B: Glossary of statistical analysis techniques

The glossary provides a brief definition of all statistical analysis techniques included in the main body of the text.

Analysis of variance (**ANOVA**) tests the main and interaction effects of categorical independent variables on an interval dependent variable (Garson).

One-way analysis of variance tests differences in a single interval dependent variable within two or more groups formed by the categories of a single categorical independent variable (Garson).

Scheffé post-hoc tests control for Type 1 errors in post-hoc testing of differences in group means. A Type 1 error arises when a researcher believes there is a relationship, but in actuality there is not (Garson).

Chi-square analysis (**χ^2**) tests for significance in the relationship between two or more categorical variables (StatSoft, Inc, 2001).

Chi-square automatic interaction detection (**CHAID**) identifies significant independent 'predictors' of group membership of the nominated dependent variable, and also examines all possible interactions between independent variables to identify separate sub-groups in the sample, introducing them at different levels.

Two-way chi-square identifies whether there is a significant relationship between two categorical or nominal independent variables.

Cluster analysis seeks to identify a set of 'homogeneous' sub-groups within a population, which both minimise intra-group variation and maximise inter-group variation (Garson).

Hierarchical cluster analysis allows clusters to be 'nested' rather than mutually exclusive as is usually the case. Therefore, a large cluster may contain a number of smaller clusters (Garson).

Factor analysis uncovers the structure of a set of variables by reducing a larger number of variables to a smaller number of dimensions or factors (Garson). Variables within a factor tend to be highly intercorrelated, but uncorrelated with variables from other factors.

Cronbach's alpha tests the internal reliability of a set of factors. If the inter-item correlations are high, there is evidence to suggest the items are measuring the same underlying construct (UCLA, Academic Technology Services, 2000). The alpha score is related to the mean of all the pairwise inter-item correlations.

Principal component analysis (PCA) seeks the set of independent factors that account for all the common and unique variance in a collection of variables (Garson).

Varimax rotation minimises the number of variables that have high loadings on any one of a set of independent factors. As a result, each factor will tend to have either large or small loadings of particular variables on it (Garson).

Multivariate analyses involve more than one dependent variable in the analysis.

Path analysis enables relationships between variables to be looked at both directly and indirectly. The same variable can act as a dependent variable at one stage of the calculation and as an independent one at another stage.

Pearson product-moment correlation (Pearson's r) is a measure of the linear relationship between two variables, both of which are measured at the interval level.

Regression analysis involves the prediction of scores on one variable by their scores on one or more other variables. It allows for specific predictions to be made about the dependent variable from the independent variable(s), and also for tests on whether the set of independent variables as a whole, or any particular independent variable, has a significant relationship with the dependent variable.

Dummy variables are used to include categorical independent variables in regression analysis. A separate dummy variable is used for each level of the variable, and coded as 1 if the variable takes that level and as 0 otherwise.

Simple linear regression sets out to establish the best straight line that accounts for the relationship between two variables.

Multiple linear regression (also referred to as **multiple regression**) extends simple linear regression by finding the linear relationship that best predicts a single dependent variable from two or more independent variables.

Logistic regression finds how best to predict, from one or more independent variables, which of two values a dichotomous dependent variable will take.

Nominal logistic regression extends logistic regression to the case where the dependent variable can take more than two values, but there is no ordering relationship between them.

Ordered logistic regression (also referred to as **ordered logit regression**) extends logistic regression to the case where the dependent variable can take more than two values, which are arranged in an ordered sequence.

Stepwise regression aims to find a subset of the total set of independent variables that predicts the dependent variable most accurately and most efficiently. It involves entering the variables one at a time, or deleting them one at a time, until no further improvement in prediction can be obtained.

Stepwise linear regression is stepwise regression applied to multiple linear regression. It aims to find the 'best' linear relationship that predicts a single dependent variable from two or more independent variables, and involves the entering or deletion of variables, one at a time, until no further improvement in prediction can be obtained.

Stepwise logistic regression is stepwise regression applied to logistic regression. It finds how best to predict, from one or more independent variables, which of two values a dichotomous dependent variable will take, and involves the entering or deletion of variables, one at a time, until no further improvement in prediction can be made.

t-test analysis (*t*)

Independent samples t-tests are used to compare two different samples that have experienced different levels of an independent variable.

Appendix C: Scaled questions and regression analyses (Chapter Two)

Table C1: Mean scaled question scores for men and women

Question	Men	Women
How well do you think you manage your money?	3.52	3.82
To what extent do you work out your incomings and outgoings?	3.14	3.52
To what extent do you keep a record of the money you spend?	2.76	3.24
To what extent do you plan ahead financially for social activities?	3.00	3.26
To what extent do you plan ahead for luxury items?	3.32	3.86
To what extent do you put money aside for emergencies?	2.18	2.56
To what extent do you delay paying one bill in order to pay another?	5.90	5.47
How often do you eat out or buy take-aways?	4.44	4.86
If you have overspent one week, to what extent do you cut back on spending the next?	3.60	3.66
To what extent do you agree with: 'I still go out even if I can't afford to'?	3.24	3.52
To what extent do you agree with: 'If I go out when money is tight, I am careful about how much I spend'?	4.12	5.22
To what extent do you agree with: 'I would spend my last £10 on a social activity, rather than put it towards an unpaid bill'?	3.64	4.70
How often do you cut back on heating the house to save money?	2.36	2.92
If money is particularly short, to what extent do you cut back on food?	3.28	3.64
How often do you ask your parents/family for extra financial help?	4.80	4.80
When you are short of money, how often do you borrow from friends?	5.40	5.78
How often do you go over your overdraft limit?	4.22	4.50

Note: Responses were recorded on 7 point scales, a score of 1 relating to poor money management (high expenditure) and a score of 7 to good money management (low expenditure).

Table C2: Regression analysis to predict money management style

Variable	B	b	t	Sig.T
Fixed income	.5917	.3260	2.714	.0100
Gender	.8583	.4843	3.839	.0005
Personal assets	–.4868	–.2669	–2.040	.0485
Student loans	.5078	.4592	2.995	.0049
Money management	.2204	.1802	1.280	ns
Credit card	.5109	.2883	2.392	.0220
Worse 'debt'	.3454	.1948	1.642	ns
Vacation work	.3614	.2488	1.872	ns
Credit and debt tolerance	–.4727	–.3109	–2.249	.0305
Savings	.2729	.2164	1.631	ns
Student loan borrowings	–.2205	–.2331	–1.521	ns
Overdraft borrowings	–.1048	–.1935	–1.256	ns
Year of study	.5611	.3161	1.934	ns

Notes: The 13 variable regression model found an overall highly significant relationship (F=13.37, df 37, p<.001) between the dependent variable – money management style – and the regressors.

B: unstandardised regression coefficients
b: the standardised regression coefficients

Table C3: Nominal logistic regressions to differentiate the three clusters

Variable	Probability
Main differences between clusters 1 and 2	
Number of accounts	.002
Whether own a credit card	.001
Whether have been overdrawn	.029
Whether set a limit to spending on a night out and keep to it	.032
Subsidiary differences between clusters 1 and 2	
Number of credit cards	.000
Main differences between clusters 2 and 3	
Whether own a credit card	.003
Whether have been overdrawn	.037
Whether try to cut down spending after an expensive week	.006
Regularity of checking bank balance	.005
Subsidiary differences between clusters 2 and 3	
Whether save money	.006
Number of credit cards	.008
Whether set a weekly spending limit	.025
Whether keep receipts	.004
Regularity of giving self-gifts	.014
Budget method 2	.046
Budget method 3	.019
Budget method 4	.016

Notes: 'Main differences' include variables that showed significant differences between clusters 1, 2 and 3 (G=150.079, *df* 12). 'Subsidiary variables' include variables that only showed significant differences when tested without the main variables (G=114.486, *df* 16). A collection of variables were not used in cluster analysis because of their continuous nature, but all were found to be insignificant when tested in a *nominal logistic regression*.

Appendix D: Davies and Lea's (1995) 14 attitude statements (Chapter Three)

1. There is no excuse for borrowing money.
2. Banks should not give interest-free overdrafts to students.
3. Students have to go into debt.
4. It is okay to borrow money in order to buy food.
5. You should always save up first before buying something.
6. Debt is an integral part of today's lifestyle.
7. Students should be discouraged from using credit cards.
8. Banks should not be surprised when students incur large debts.
9. It is okay to have an overdraft if you know you can pay it off.
10. Once you are in debt it is very difficult to get out.
11. You should stay home rather than borrow money to go out for an evening in the pub.
12. It is better to have something now and pay for it later.
13. Taking out a loan is a good thing because it allows you to enjoy life as a student.
14. Owing money is basically wrong.

Appendix E: Factor analysis and multiple regression (Chapter Four)

Table E1: Factor analysis of 11 of the 14 items from the Davies and Lea (1995) attitude scale

Statement	Mean	F1	F2
It is better to have something now and pay for it later	3.19	.70	
You should always save up first before buying something	4.48	.68	
Taking out a loan is a good thing because it allows you to enjoy student life	4.53	.67	
You should stay home rather than borrow money to go out for an evening in the pub	4.48	.65	
Owing money is basically wrong	2.63	.57	
There is no excuse for borrowing money	1.70	.57	
Banks should not give interest-free overdrafts to students	1.71	.50	
Students have to go into debt	4.88		.74
Banks should not be surprised when students incur large debts	5.98		.62
Debt is an integral part of today's lifestyle	5.02	.36	.59
Students should be discouraged from using credit cards	5.21	.39	–.59

Notes: Responses were given on a 7 point scale with endpoints labelled 1 'strongly disagree' and 7 'strongly agree'. Factor analysis was repeated with 11 of the 14 statements because three did not load highly on either of the two factors identified. Two factors accounting for 43% (27% Factor 1, 16% Factor 2) of the variance were rotated to a *varimax* solution. Factors with loadings less than .30 have been suppressed to aid interpretation.

Table E2: Multiple linear regression to predict acceptability of credit and debt

Variable	B	b	Sig.T
Gender	–.18833	–.10642	.1243
Student loans	.00018	.40075***	.0000
All other borrowings	–.00000	.00058	.9936
		R=.433*** R^2=.187	

Notes: The *multiple linear regression* was significantly different from zero. The combined independent variables predicted 18.7% of the variance, and collectively had a significant relationship with the dependent variable (F=13.59, df 3, p<.001).

B: unstandardised regression coefficients
b: the standardised regression coefficients
R: the multiple correlation
R^2: the squared multiple correlation
*** p<.001

Appendix F: Factor analysis (Chapter Five)

Table F1: Factor analysis of the sources of 'money troubles'

Sources	Mean	F1	F2
Careless budgeting	4.37	.80	
Lack of self-discipline	4.23	.79	
Not being good with money	4.02	.78	
Not economising when necessary	4.42	.71	
The ease of obtaining credit	3.82	.63	
High credit limits	3.33	.62	
Wanting to have a good time	5.60	.55	
Enjoyment of shopping	3.97	.55	
Convenience of using credit cards	3.62	.54	
Impulse buying	4.18	.53	
Being under stress	3.70		.72
Being unhappy	2.81		.66
The high cost of living	4.68		.64
High interest rates	2.81		.61
Illness	2.17		.61
Not enough money for day to day living	4.10		.53
Bad luck	2.90		.49

Notes: Responses were on a 7 point scale with endpoints labelled 1 'unlikely' and 7 'likely'. Items were then factor analysed (KMO= 816, Bartlett=.000) and two factors accounting for 41% of the variance were rotated to a *varimax* solution. Items with low final commonalities (<. 25) were omitted and are not reported here.

Index

[Page numbers in italics indicate table or figure]

K

L

M

O

P

R

S